Benchmark ADVANCE®

Phonics and Word Recognition

W9-AYB-373

Grades 4-6

About *Benchmark Advance* Intervention

Benchmark Advance Intervention is intended for students who need extra support to master grade-level skills. It offers reteaching and additional practice to reinforce instruction in the core program. *Benchmark Advance* Intervention provides direct instruction of the Foundational Skills, Grades K–5. The skills are addressed as shown below.

Grade **K**	Grade **1**	Grade **2**	Grade **3**	Grades **4–6**
Print Concepts	**Print Concepts**	**Print Concepts**	**Print Concepts**	**Phonics and Word Recognition**
Phonological Awareness	**Phonological Awareness**	**Phonological Awareness**	**Phonological Awareness**	**Fluency**
Phonics and Word Recognition	**Phonics and Word Recognition**	**Phonics and Word Recognition**	**Phonics and Word Recognition**	
Fluency	**Fluency**	**Fluency**	**Fluency**	

At Grades K–3, individual grade-level packages of lessons and blackline masters address all of the Foundational skills. An additional package for Grades 4–6 addresses the Phonics and Word Recognition and Fluency skills for Grades 2–5. In addition, each of the packages at Grades K–3 includes lessons and blackline masters to address the Foundational skills presented in previous grades. In this way, teachers can address the needs of students at each student's instructional level—whether at/near grade level or below.

The program offers skill-focused sequential and systematic instruction that is parallel to instruction in the core program. Each lesson is designed to target a specific skill that needs bolstering as revealed through program assessments.

It can be implemented flexibly in small groups or to individual students. Each lesson is designed to be completed in 15 minutes.

Lesson Structure

All of the phonics and word recognition lessons in *Benchmark Advance* Intervention follow a consistent instructional design that offers explicit skills instruction and a gradual release model to scaffold student learning.

The side column at the start of every lesson furnishes the information teachers need to manage student learning:

- The specific lesson objective that states what students will be able to do after completing the lesson
- The metacognitive strategy that students will use as they learn
- The essential academic language and materials that students will use in the lesson are listed
- A reminder of the prerequisite skills that students need to fully understand the lesson

The instructional lessons offer consistent and explicit instruction that helps students focus on the specific lesson objectives:

- The Introduce and State Learning Goal sections set the learning goal for the lesson.
- The Teach and Model sections of the lesson feature direct instruction and teacher modeling, including phonemic awareness and sound/spelling correspondence.
- The Practice and Apply sections offer guided and independent practice of the focus skill including practice reading high-frequency words and decodable text, and writing spelling words.
- The Conclusion gives students an opportunity to restate what they've learned in the lesson.
- The Home Connection sidebar links the lesson to at-home practice within the family setting.

Every lesson ends with a point-of-use formative assessment so teachers can evaluate whether students have mastered the target skills. Intervention 2 suggestions provide alternative teaching ideas for working with students who need further support.

The blackline masters that accompany the lessons provide practice and application opportunities to promote mastery.

Corrective Feedback

Inherent in the teaching profession is the need to make corrections. In both structural and communicative approaches to language teaching and learning, feedback is viewed as a means of fostering learner motivation and ensuring linguistic accuracy (Ellis 2009). The purpose of the feedback is to close the gap between the student's current learning status and the lesson goals (Sadler 1989). Students can receive feedback in three ways: from their teachers, from peers, and through self-assessment.

Formative assessment is a process that teachers and students use during instruction. It provides feedback to inform ongoing teaching and learning approaches. Corrective feedback is also an essential feature of language development instruction. Teachers provide students with judiciously selected corrective feedback on language usage in ways that are transparent and meaningful to students. Overcorrection or arbitrary corrective feedback is avoided.

Corrective feedback is information given to learners regarding a linguistic error they have made (Loewen 2012; Sheen 2007). The feedback information can consist of any one or all of the following:

(a) **an indication that an error has been committed,**

(b) **provision of the correct target language form, or**

(c) **metalinguistic information about the nature of the error.**

Corrective feedback in the form of negotiating for meaning can help learners notice their errors and create meaningful connections, thus aiding acquisition. It is important to emphasize that language learners can only self-correct if they possess the necessary linguistic knowledge (Ellis 2003).

One solution sometimes advocated to this problem is to conduct corrective feedback as a two-stage process: first encourage self- correction and then, if that fails, provide the correction (Doughty and Varela 1998).

Corrective feedback can be:

Explicit
Corrective feedback overtly draws the learner's attention to the error made.

Implicit
Corrective feedback focuses the learner's attention without overtly informing the learner that he/she has made an error or interrupting the flow of interaction.

Corrective Feedback Strategies

	IMPLICIT Attracts learner's attention without overtly informing the learner that he/she has made an error or interrupting the flow of interaction.	EXPLICIT Tries to overtly draw the learner's attention to the error made.
INPUT PROVIDING: **Correct form is given to students.**	**RECAST** The teacher incorporates the content words of the immediately preceding incorrect utterance and changes and corrects the utterance in some way (e.g., phonological, syntactic, morphological, or lexical). L: I went school. T: You went to school?	**EXPLICIT CORRECTION** The teacher indicates an error has been committed, identifies the error, and provides the correction. L: We will go on May. T: Not *on* May, *in* May. T: We will go in May.
OUTPUT PROMPTING: **The student is prompted to self-correct.**	**REPETITION** The teacher repeats the learner utterance highlighting the error by means of emphatic stress. L: I will showed you. T: I will *show* you. L: I will show you.	**METALINGUISTIC EXPLANATION** The teacher provides explanation for the errors that have been made. L: two duck T: Do you remember how to show more than one duck? L: ducks T: Yes, you remember that we need to add "s" at the end of a noun to show the plural form.
	CLARIFICATION REQUEST The teacher indicates that he/she has not understood what the learner said. L: on the it go T: Can you please tell me again? T: Do you mean "it goes on your desk"?	**ELICITATION** The teacher repeats part of the learner utterance, but not the erroneous part and uses rising intonation to signal the learner should complete it. L: I don't think won't rain. T: I don't think it …(will) rain.
		PARALINGUISTIC SIGNAL The teacher uses a gesture or facial expression to indicate that the learner has made an error. L: Yesterday I go to the movies. T: (gestures with right forefinger over left shoulder to indicate past)

Adapted from: Ellis, Rod. "Corrective Feedback and Teacher Development." L2 Journal, volume 1 (2009).

Recommendations for English Learners

	Student Language and Literacy Characteristics	Considerations for Instructions
Oral Skills	**No or little spoken English proficiency**	**Students will need instruction in recognizing and distinguishing the sounds of English as compared or contrasted with sounds in their native language.** • Use visuals and gestures to convey that in English, letters are symbols that represent sounds and that words are a sequence of letters that make up a word that conveys meaning.

	Oral skills: Spoken English proficiency	**Students will need instruction in applying their knowledge of the English sound system to foundational literacy learning.**
		
		• Take an inventory of students' oral vocabulary. Draw upon students' known and familiar oral vocabulary to:
		
		   • Clap syllables in known words.
		
		   • Segment and blend syllables of known words.
		
		   • Listen to the sequence of sounds in known words.
		
		   • Use Visuals to support comprehension.

Print Skills	**No or little native language literacy**	**Students will need instruction in print concepts.**
		
		• As students develop an understanding of the organization and basic features of print, they learn that spoken words in English are composed of smaller elements of speech and that letters represent these sounds (alphabetical principle).
		
		• Instruction systematically includes:
		
		   1 Following words from left to right, top to bottom, and page by page.
		
		   2. Recognizing that spoken words are represented in written language by specific sequences of letters.
		
		   3. Understanding that words are separated by spaces in print.
		
		   4. Recognizing and naming all upper- and lowercase letters of the alphabet.
		
		   5. Recognizing the distinguishing features of a sentence (e.g., first word, capitalization, ending punctuation).

	Some foundational literacy proficiency in a language not using the Latin alphabet
	
	(e.g., Arabic, Chinese, Korean, Russian)
		Students will be familiar with print concepts, and will need instruction in learning the Latin alphabet for English, as compared or contrasted with their native language writing system (e.g., direction of print, symbols representing whole words, syllables or phonemes).
		
		• For students who have been taught to use a logographic system, an introduction to the alphabet is necessary and the instruction needs to include sound-symbol relationships (Chinese languages, Korean).
		
		• For students who use an alphabetic language that does not use the Latin alphabet, an introduction to the alphabet is necessary and the instruction needs to include sound-symbol relationships (Greek, Arabic, Russian).
		
		• Compare and contrast directionality and print orientation:
		
		   • Left to right, top to bottom: Greek, Russian, Brahmic, Thai
		
		   • Right-to-left orientation, top to bottom: Arabic, Hebrew, Persian, Syriac, Urdu

	Some foundational literacy proficiency in a language using the Latin alphabet (e.g., Spanish)	**Students will need instruction in applying their knowledge of print concepts, phonics and word recognition to the English writing system, as compared or contrasted with their native language alphabet (e.g., letters that are the same or different, or represent the same or different sounds) and native language vocabulary (e.g., cognates) and sentence structure (e.g., subject-verb-object vs. subject-object-verb word order).** • Most languages that use the Latin alphabet have the same line direction (left to right) and same block direction (top to bottom). (English, Spanish, French, Portuguese)

Identify and Decode Irregular Plural Nouns

Introduce

As students participate in this lesson, they will identify and spell irregular plural nouns.

State Learning Goal

Say: *Today we will practice identifying and spelling plural nouns that do not end in* **s**.

Teach

Say: *Most of the time we form plural nouns by adding* **s**, **es**, *or* **ies** *to the end of words (vines, pouches, ponies). But other times plural nouns have irregular spellings. They do not have an* **s** *at the end. We change letters in the word to make them plural.*

Ask: *What is the plural of* **foot?** **(feet)**

Say: *Sometimes they do not change at all. What is the plural of* **sheep?** **(sheep)**

Phonemic Awareness

Display the irregular singular/plural pair **woman/women**.

Say: *Listen to the vowel sound in woman.* /w/ /o/ /m/ /a/ /n/

Say: *Now listen to the vowel sound in women.* /w/ /o/ /m/ /e/ /n/

Sound-Spelling Correspondence

Display the irregular plurals **child/children**.

Say: *The singular form of this noun is* **child**, *but the plural form is* **children**. *Notice that the plural has* /r/ /e/ /n/ *at the end.*

Model

Use BLM 1, Row 1.

Say: *We will look at each picture. Say its name.*

Ask: *What do you see in the first picture? (a* **hoof**)

Say: *We make the singular noun* **hoof** *plural by changing the* **f** *to a* **v** *and adding* **-es**. *Write the plural noun* **hooves** *on the line.*

Repeat with other words.

Practice

Use BLM 1, Row 2.

Say: *Look at each picture. Say its name. If a noun is plural, we will write its singular form on the line. If a noun is singular, we will write its plural form on the line.*

Say: *The first picture shows* **men**. *It is the plural form of the noun* **man**. *Write* **man** *on the line.*

Lesson Objectives

- Identify and name plural nouns.
- Learn rules for spelling irregular plural nouns.

Metacognitive Strategy
- Selective Auditory Attention
- Imagery
- Auditory Representation

Academic Language
- irregular, plural, noun

Additional Materials
- Blackline Master 1

Pre-Assess
Student's ability to recognize the rules for forming irregular plural nouns and know that plural nouns mean more than one

Apply

Blend Words

Use BLM 1, Row 3.

Say: *Look at each letter of the first word and listen to the sound as I read.* /t/ /ē/ /th/ *Your turn:* /t/ /ē/ /th/.

Say: *Now we are going to blend the sounds together by stretching them out as we read them.* Point to each letter in a sweeping motion left to right /teeeth/.

Ask: *What is the word?* (**teeth**)

Spelling

Use BLM 1, Row 4.

Say: *Now we can practice writing the sounds we hear in each word. Say one word at a time, stretching each sound.*

Say: *Say the word slowly; write a letter for each sound you hear.*

Conclusion

Say: *What did we learn today? We learned that many plural nouns have irregular spellings and that there are some basic rules to help us know how to spell them.*

Home Connection

Encourage students to practice identifying irregularly spelled plural nouns. Encourage students to identify other irregularly spelled plural nouns with their families.

✔ Formative Assessment

If the student completes each task correctly, proceed to the next skill in the sequence. If not, refer to suggested Intervention 2.

Did the student...?	Intervention 2
Identify the name of the letters?	• Use physical rhythmic movements as the letter name is repeated. March while chanting the letter name. Move arms up and down. Sway from side to side.
Identify the sounds of the letters?	• Have students practice identifying words using tactile letters and pictures. As students touch the initial vowels in the word, have them repeat the short vowel sound.
Produce the sounds of the letters?	• Say a short vowel sound aloud multiple times and ask students to put their hands on their head when they hear you alternate to the long vowel sound. Then switch roles.
Recognize the final sounds?	• Use Elkonin boxes – students move a token into the last box as the final sound of the word is said.
Write the letters?	• Write the letter, have students trace it. Create the letter with clay. • Discuss letter features (lines, shape). Trace over the letter with multiple colors.
Know the name of pictures?	• Tell students the name of pictures, have students repeat them aloud. Discuss word and use each word in context.

Recognize Open Syllables

Introduce

As students participate in this lesson, they will identify open syllables. Students will apply their knowledge by recognizing words containing open syllables using pictures. Students will apply this skill in context by reading decodable simple sentences that include high frequency words.

State Learning Goal

Say: *Today we will learn to read words that have open syllables.*

Teach

Say: *An open syllable has a vowel sound as the last sound. To say a syllable that ends in a vowel, we have to end the syllable with our mouths open. Usually, the vowel sound in an open syllable is a long vowel sound: /a/ /e/ /i/ /o/ /u/.*

Phonemic Awareness

Say: *Listen to this word:* **he**. *The last letter in this word is* **e**. *The last sound in this word is long /ē/. We finish saying it with our mouths open.* **He** *is a word with one syllable. That syllable is an open syllable.*

Sound-Spelling Correspondence

Write and display the sound /ā/ and the letters **ai** and **ay**, as well as the sound /ē/ and the letters **ee**, **ie**, and **ea**.

Say: *Each long vowel sound has different letters that spell that sound.*

Say: *For example, the long sound /ā/ can be formed by different letter combinations, such as* **ai** *and* **ay**. *Say the sound with me: /ā/.*

Say: *The long sound /ē/ can be formed by different letter combinations, such as* **ee**, **ie**, *and* **ea**. *Say the sound with me: /ē/.*

Say: *Open syllables end with vowel sounds. These sounds can be formed by different letters.*

Model

Use BLM 2, Row 1.

Say: *We will look at each picture. We will say its name. Listen for the open syllable. If we hear the open syllable, we will circle the picture. If we do not hear the open syllable, we will cross out the picture.*

Ask: *What do you see in the first picture?* (**me**). *Do you hear the open syllable in the word* **me**? *Circle the picture. If you do not hear the open syllable, then cross out the picture.*

Lesson Objectives

- Produce open syllables.
- Relate open syllables to the letters that make them.
- Recognize open syllables words and pictures.
- Write letters and letter combinations that make open syllables.
- Read common high frequency words: **have, my, you, one.**

Metacognitive Strategy
- Selective Auditory Attention
- Imagery
- Auditory Representation

Academic Language
- vowel, long vowel sound, vowel team

Additional Materials
- Sound Spelling Cards for **a**, **ai**, **ay**, **e**, **y**, **ey**
- Blackline Master 2

Pre-Assess

Student's ability to recognize the open syllables represented by the corresponding letters and vowel teams. Ability to pronounce the long vowel sound /e/.

Practice

Use BLM 2, Row .2

Say: *Look at the picture. Say its name. Listen for the open syllable.*

Ask: *What do you see in the first picture?* **(cry)** *Do you hear the open syllable in the word* **hi**? *What is the vowel sound in the open syllable?* /ī/

Say: *What letter or letters make the long sound* /ī/ *in the open syllable? Write the letter or letters that make the sound* /ī/ *in the open syllable on the line under each picture.*

Apply

Blend Words

Use BLM 2, Row 3.

Say: *Look at the word and listen for the open syllable as I read.* /s/ /p/ /ī/ /d/ /er/ *Your turn:* /s/ /p/ /ī/ /d/ /er/

Say: *Now we are going to blend the sounds together by stretching them out as we read them.* Point to each letter in a sweeping motion left to right /ssspīīder/.

Ask: *What word?* **(spider)**

Spelling

Use BLM 2, Row 4.

Say: *Now we can practice writing the sounds we hear in each word. Call one word at a time, stretching each sound.*

Say: *Say the word slowly; write a letter for each sound you hear.*

Conclusion

Say: *What did we learn today? We learned that open syllables end in a long vowel sound. We learned that long vowel sounds can be formed by different letters.*

Home Connection

Ask students to practice identifying open syllables with a family member. Have students identify other words that include open syllables with their family.

✔ Formative Assessment

If the student completes each task correctly, proceed to the next skill in the sequence. If not, refer to suggested Intervention 2.

Did the student…?	Intervention 2
Identify open syllables?	• Model saying open and closed syllables while students focus on the position of your mouth. Then have students identify open vowel sounds based on your mouth position. Ask them to repeat the open syllable after you.
Identify the sounds in the open syllables?	• Use sound/spelling cards to review each long vowel sound and its different spellings
Produce the vowel sounds?	• Use mirrors to show the movement of the mouth, tongue, and teeth as the sound is produced. Use hand over mouth to explore movement of air as the sound is produced.
Know the names of pictures?	• Tell students the name of pictures, have student repeat it aloud. • Discuss meaning of word. Use word in context.
Read high-frequency words?	• Create take home word cards. Use a reward system to track words known over time. Student uses the word in a sentence, teacher writes it down and highlights the word. Sentence is re-read the next day.

Identify and Name Closed Syllables

Introduce

As students participate in this lesson, they will identify closed syllables in two-syllable words, and identify syllables when the sound and name is given orally. Students will apply their knowledge by recognizing the sound of closed syllables using pictures. Students will apply the skill in context by reading simple decodable sentences that include high frequency words.

State Learning Goal

Say: *Words are made up of syllables. Each vowel sound makes a syllable. In closed syllables, the vowel is followed by a consonant.*

Teach

Say: *Letters represent sounds. We remember the sounds each letter makes. Letters are divided into vowels and consonants. Every syllable contains a vowel sound. A closed syllable starts with a vowel and ends with a consonant. The vowel in a closed syllable has a short sound. It does not say its name.*

Phonemic Awareness

Say: *Listen to this word:* **win***. Say it with me:* **win***. Say it on your own:* **win***.*

Sound-Spelling Correspondence

Show the letters.

Say: *The word* **win** *is one syllable.*

Say: *The word* **win** *is a closed syllable.*

Ask: *How many syllables?* (**one**) *What kind of syllable?* (**closed**)

Model

Use BLM 3, Row 1.

Say: *Look at each picture. Say its name.* **Listen for the closed syllables.**

Ask: *Look at the first picture. Do you hear the closed syllable in the word* **trumpet***? If we hear the closed syllables, we will circle the picture with the trumpet. If we do not hear a closed syllables, we cross out the picture.*

Lesson Objectives

- Identify closed syllables.
- Produce the sound of closed syllables.
- Recognize closed syllables in words/pictures.
- Read common high frequency words: **jump, want, put, what.**

Metacognitive Strategy
- Selective Auditory Attention
- Imagery
- Auditory Representation

Academic Language
- vowel, closed syllable

Additional Materials
- Blackline Master 3

Pre-Assess
Student's ability to recognize the sound represented by a syllable and to identify the letters used to represent the corresponding sound.

Practice

Use BLM 3, Row 2.

Say: *Look at the word. Say its name. Write the letters.*

Say: *Look at the first word. (***pencil***) Do you hear the two closed syllables in the word* **pencil**? *Circle the two syllables:* **pen/cil**.

Apply
Blend Words

Use BLM 3, Row 3.

Say: *Look at each letter and listen to the sound as I read.* **/b/ /u/ /t/ /er/**. *Your turn:* **/b/ /u/ /t/ /er/**.

Say: *Now we are going to blend the sounds together by stretching them out as we read them.* Point to each letter in a sweeping motion left to right **/buuuter/**.

Ask: *What word? (***butter***)*

Spelling

Use BLM 3, Row 4.

Say: *Now we can practice writing the sounds we hear in each word. Call one word at a time, stretching each sound.*

Say: *Say the word slowly; write a letter for each sound you hear.*

Conclusion

Ask: *What did we learn today? We learned that words are made of syllables. Closed syllables have a vowel followed by a consonant. What pictures/words will help you remember closed two-syllable words?*

✔ Formative Assessment

If the student completes each task correctly, proceed to the next skill in the sequence. If not, refer to suggested Intervention 2.

Did the student…?	Intervention 2
Identify the name of the letters?	• Use physical rhythmic movements as the letter name is repeated. March while chanting the letter name. Move arms up and down. Sway from side to side.
Identify the sounds of the letters?	• Use alliteration, chants that repeat the sound several times then a word that begins with the sound.
Produce the sounds of the letters?	• Use mirrors to show the movement of the mouth, tongue, and teeth as the sound is produced • Use hand over mouth to explore movement of air as the sound is produced.
Recognize the syllables?	• Use Elkonin boxes – students move a token into the box as each syllable in the word is said.
Write the letters?	• Write the letter, have students trace it. Create letter with clay. • Discuss letter features (lines, shape). Trace over letter with multiple colors.
Know the names of pictures?	• Tell students the name of pictures, have student repeat them aloud. • Discuss meaning of word. Use word in context.
Read high-frequency words?	• Create take-home word cards. Use a reward system to track words known over time. Student uses the word in a sentence, teacher writes it down and highlights HFW. The student re-reads it the next day.

Identify and Name Vowel Teams
o͞o and o͝o

Introduce

As students participate in this lesson, they will identify the name and sound of the target letter, and they will identify the letter when the sound and name is given orally. Students will apply their knowledge by recognizing the sound of target letters using pictures.

State Learning Goal

Say: *The letter o is a vowel. When we double letter oo, we can form two sounds, the /o͞o/ and /o͝o/ sound. Today we will listen to the oo vowel team sounds in the middle of words.*

Teach

Say: *Letters represent sounds. We remember the sounds each letter makes. We use letters to write words we say. We use letters to read and write words. The letter o is a vowel. When doubled, the letter forms two sounds: /o͞o/ and /o͝o/.*

Phonemic Awareness

Show picture of sound/spelling card to review the sound of /o͞o/ and /o͝o/.

Say: *Listen to this sound /o͞o/. Say it with me: /o͞o/. Say it on your own: /o͞o/.*

Repeat for the sound of /o͞o/.

Sound-Spelling Correspondence

Show the letter.

Say: *The way we write the sounds /o͞o/ and /o͝o/ is with the letters oo.*

Say: *The letters oo make the sound /o͞o/ and /o͝o/.*

Ask: *What is the name of the letters? oo What are the sounds the letters oo make? /o͞o/ and /o͝o/.*

Model

Use BLM 4, Row 1.

Say: *Look at each picture. Say its name. Listen for the sound of /o͝o/ in the middle.*

Say: *Look at the first picture. Do you hear the sound /o͝o/ in the middle of the word book? If we hear the sound of /o͝o/ in the middle of the word, we will circle the picture of the book. If we do not hear the sound /o͝o/ in the middle, we will cross out the picture.*

Lesson Objectives

- Identify and name the letters **oo**.
- Produce the sound of letters **oo**.
- Relate the sound /o͞o/ and /o͝o/ to the letters **oo**.
- Recognize vowel team sound **/oo/** and **/oo/** in words/pictures.

Metacognitive Strategy
- Selective Auditory Attention
- Imagery
- Auditory Representation

Academic Language
- letter name, letter sound, vowel, short sound, vowel team, middle

Additional Materials
- Sound Spelling Card **oo**
- Blackline Master 4

Pre-Assess
Student's ability to recognize the sound represented by the target letter of the alphabet and to identify the letter used to represent the corresponding sound.

Practice

Use BLM 4, Row 2.

Say: *Look at the word. Say its name.*

Say: *Look at the first word.* (**look**) *Do you hear the sound /o͝o/ in the middle of the word **look**? Then write the letters **oo**. Repeat for /o͞o/ with the word **pool**. Write the letters **oo** on the lines.*

Apply

Blend Words

Use BLM 4, Row 3.

Say: *Look at each letter and listen to the sound as I read:* **/h/ /o͞o/ /k/.** *Your turn:* **/h/ /o͞o/ /k/.**

Say: *Now we are going to blend the sounds together by stretching them out as we read them.* *Point to each letter in a sweeping motion left to right* **/ho͝ook/.**

Ask: *What word?* (**hook**)

Repeat for **groom** and **cartoon**.

Spelling

Use BLM 4, Row 4.

Say: *Now we can practice writing the sounds we hear in each word. Call one word at a time, stretching each sound.*

Say: *Say the word slowly; write a letter for each sound you hear.*

Conclusion

Ask: *What did we learn today? We learned that the letters oo make the sounds /o͞o/ and /o͝o/ in the middle of some words. What pictures/words will help you remember the sounds /o͞o/ and /o͝o/ and the letters **oo**?*

Home Connection

Encourage students to practice identifying the medial vowel team sound and writing the letters **oo** with a family member. Encourage students to identify other words that have either a medial /o͞o/ or /o͝o/ vowel sound with their families.

✔ Formative Assessment

If the student completes each task correctly, proceed to the next skill in the sequence. If not, refer to suggested Intervention 2.

Did the student…?	Intervention 2
Identify the name of the letters?	• Use physical rhythmic movements as the letter name is repeated. March while chanting the letter name. Move arms up and down. Sway from side to side.
Identify the sounds of the letters?	• Use exaggeration of forming the letters oo by bringing the lips together in a pucker.
Produce the sounds of the letters?	• Use mirrors to show the movement of the mouth, tongue, and teeth as the sound is produced. • Use hand over mouth to explore movement of air as the sound is produced.
Recognize the middle sounds?	• Use Elkonin boxes – student moves a token into the middle boxes as the middle sound of the word is said.
Write the letters?	• Write the letter, have students trace it. Create letter with clay. • Discuss letter features (lines, shape). Trace over letter with multiple colors.
Know the names of pictures?	• Tell students the name of pictures, have student repeat it aloud. • Discuss meaning of word. Use word in context.

Identify and Name Vowel Team ou

Introduce

As students participate in this lesson, they will identify the name and sound of the target letter, and they will identify the letter when the sound and name is given orally. Students will apply their knowledge by recognizing the sound of target letters using pictures.

State Learning Goal

Say: *The letters* **o** *and* **u** *are vowels. They form one sound: the /ou/ sound. Today we will listen to this vowel team sound in the middle of words.*

Teach

Say: *Letters represent sounds. We remember the sounds each letter makes. We use letters to write words we say. We use letters to read and write words. The letters* **o** *and* **u** *are vowels. The two vowels form one sound: /ou/. The letter* **w** *is a consonant. The letters* **o** *and* **w** *also form the /ou/ sound.*

Phonemic Awareness

Show picture of sound/spelling card to review the sound of /**ou**/.

Say: *Listen to this sound /ou/. Say it with me: /ou/. Say it on your own: /ou/.*

Sound-Spelling Correspondence

Show the letter.

Say: *The way we write the sound /ou/ is with the letters* **ou** *or* **ow**.

Say: *The letters* **ou** *and ow make the sound /ou/.*

Say: *What is the name of the letters?* **ou** *and* **ow**. *What is the sound the letters ou or ow make?* **/ou/**

Model

Use BLM 5, Row 1.

Say: *Look at each picture. Say its name. Listen for the sound of /ou/ in the middle.*

Say: *Look at the first picture. Do you hear the sound /ou/ in the middle of the word* **pout***? If we hear the sound of* **ou** *in the middle of the word, we will circle the picture. If we do not hear the sound /ou/ in the middle of the word, we will cross out the picture.*

Repeat for the words **clown** and **sound**.

Lesson Objectives

- Identify and name the letters **ou** and **ow.**
- Produce the sound of letters **ou** and **ow.**
- Relate the sound /**ou**/ to the letters **ou** and **ow.**
- Recognize **vowel team** sound **ou** in words/pictures.

Metacognitive Strategy
- Selective Auditory Attention
- Imagery
- Auditory Representation

Academic Language
- letter name, letter sound, vowel, short sound, vowel team, middle

Additional Materials
- Sound Spelling Card **ou**
- Blackline Master 5

Pre-Assess
Student's ability to recognize the sound represented by the target letter of the alphabet and to identify the letter used to represent the corresponding sound.

Practice

Use BLM 5, Row 2.

Say: *Look at the picture. Say its name. Write the letter.*

Say: *What is shown by the first picture? (a **mouse**) Do you hear the sound /**ou**/ in the **middle** of the word **mouse**? Then write the letters **ou** on the line.*

Repeat for the words **frown** and **town**.

Apply

Blend Words

Use BLM 5, Row 3.

Say: *Look at each letter and listen to the sound as I read: /**m**/ /**ou**/ /**s**/. Your turn: /**m**/ /**ou**/ /**s**/.*

Say: *Now we are going to blend the sounds together by stretching them out as we read them: /**mmmooouuusss**/. What word? (**mouse**)*

Repeat for the word **town**.

Spelling

Use BLM 5, Row 4

Say: *Now we can practice writing the sounds we hear in each word.*

Call one word at a time, stretching each sound.

Say: *Say the word slowly; write a letter for each sound you hear.*

Conclusion

Ask: *What did we learn today? We learned that the letters **ou** and **ow** make the sound /**ou**/ in the middle of some words. What pictures/words will help you remember the sound /**ou**/ and the letters **ou** and **ow**?*

Home Connection

Encourage students to practice identifying the medial vowel team sound and writing the letters **ou** and **ow** with a family member. Encourage students to identify other words that have a medial /**ou**/ vowel sound with their families.

✔ Formative Assessment

If the student completes each task correctly, proceed to the next skill in the sequence. If not, refer to suggested Intervention 2.

Did the student…?	Intervention 2
Identify the name of the letters?	• Use physical rhythmic movements as the letter name is repeated. March while chanting the letter name. Move arms up and down. Sway from side to side.
Identify the sounds of the letters?	• Use exaggeration of forming the /**ou**/ by opening the mouth wide and bringing the lips together in a pucker.
Produce the sounds of the letters?	• Use mirrors to show the movement of the mouth, tongue, and teeth as the sound is produced. • Use hand over mouth to explore movement of air as the sound is produced.
Recognize the middle sounds?	• Use Elkonin boxes – student moves a token into the middle boxes as the middle sound of the word is said.
Write the letters?	• Write the letters, have students trace them. Create letters with clay. Discuss letter features (lines, shape). Trace over letters with multiple colors.
Know the names of pictures?	• Tell students the names of pictures, have students repeat them aloud. • Discuss meaning of word. Use word in context.

Identify and Name Vowel Team oi

Introduce

As students participate in this lesson, they will identify the name and sound of the target letter, and they will identify the letter when the sound and name is given orally. Students will apply their knowledge by recognizing the sound of target letters using pictures.

State Learning Goal

Say: *The letters* **o, i,** *and* **y** *are vowels. The letters* **oi** *and* **oy** *each form one sound. The* /**oi**/ *sound. Today we will listen to the vowel team sound in the middle of words.*

Teach

Say: *Letters represent sounds. We remember the sounds each letter makes. We use letters to read and write words. We know the sounds* **o** *can make and the sounds* **i** *can make, but together, they make the sound* /**oi**/*. We also know the sound* **y** *can make, and together,* **o** *and* **y** *also make the sound* /**oi**/*.

Phonemic Awareness

Show picture of sound/spelling card to review the sound of /**oi**/.

Say: *Listen to this sound* /**oi**/*. Say it with me:* /**oi**/*. Say it on your own:* /**oi**/*.

Sound-Spelling Correspondence

Show the letter.

Say: *The way we write the sound* /**oi**/ *is with the letters* **oi** *or* **oy**.

Say: *The letters* **oi** *and* **oy** *make the sound* /**oi**/*.

Ask: *What is the name of the letters?* **oi** *or* **oy** *What is the sound the letters* **oi** *or* **oy** *make?* /**oi**/

Model

Use BLM 6, Row 1.

Say: *Look at each picture. Say its name. Listen for the sound of* /**oi**/ *in the middle.*

Say: *Look at the first picture. Do you hear the sound* /**oi**/ *in the middle of the word* **coin**? *If we hear the sound of* **oi** *in the middle of the word, we will circle the picture* **coin**. *If we do not hear the sound* /**oi**/ *in the middle of the word, we will cross out the picture.*

Repeat with the word **boy**.

Lesson Objectives

- Identify and name the letters **oi** and **oy.**
- Produce the sound of letters **oi** and **oy**
- Relate the sound /**oi**/ to the letters **oi** or **oy.**
- Recognize vowel team sound **oi** in words/pictures.

Metacognitive Strategy
- Selective Auditory Attention
- Imagery
- Auditory representation

Academic Language
- letter name, letter sound, vowel, short sound, vowel team, middle

Additional Materials
- Sound Spelling Card **oi, oy**
- Blackline Master 6

Pre-Assess
Student's ability to recognize the sound represented by the target letter of the alphabet and to identify the letter used to represent the corresponding sound.

Practice

Use BLM 6, Row 2.

Say: *Look at the picture. Say its name. Trace the letter.*

Say: *What is shown by the first picture? (**coil**) Do you hear the sound /oi/ in the middle of the word* **coil***? Then trace the letters* **oi***.*

Repeat with the word **toy**.

Apply

Blend Words

Use BLM 6, Row 3.

Say: *Look at each letter and listen to the sound as I read: /oi/ /l/. Your turn: /oi/ /l/.*

Say: *Now we are going to blend the sounds together by stretching them out as we read them.* Point to each letter in a sweeping motion left to right: **/oooiiilll/**.

Ask: *What word? (**oil**)*

Repeat for the word **joy**.

Spelling

Use BLM 6, Row 4.

Say: *Now we can practice writing the sounds we hear in each word. Call one word at a time, stretching each sound.*

Say: *Say the word slowly; write a letter for each sound you hear.*

Conclusion

Ask: *What did we learn today? We learned that the letters* **oi** *and* **oy** *make the sound /oi/ in the middle of some words. What pictures/words will help you remember the sound /oi/ and the letters* **oi** *and* **oy***?*

Home Connection

Encourage students to practice identifying the medial vowel team sound and writing the letters **oi** and **oy** with a family member. Encourage students to identify other words that have a medial /oi/ vowel sound with their family.

✔ Formative Assessment

If the student completes each task correctly, proceed to the next skill in the sequence. If not, refer to suggested Intervention 2.

Did the student…?	Intervention 2
Identify the name of the letters?	• Use physical rhythmic movements as the letter name is repeated. March while chanting the letter name. Move arms up and down. Sway from side to side.
Identify the sounds of the letters?	• Use exaggeration of forming the letters **oi** and **oy** by bringing the lips together in a pucker.
Produce the sounds of the letters?	• Use mirrors to show the movement of the mouth, tongue, and teeth as the sound is produced. • Use hand over mouth to explore movement of air as the sound is produced.
Recognize the middle sounds?	• Use Elkonin boxes – student moves a token into the middle boxes as the middle sound of the word is said.
Write the letters?	• Write the letters, have students trace them. Create letters with clay. Discuss letter features (lines, shape). Trace over letters with multiple colors.
Know the name of pictures?	• Tell students the names of pictures, have students repeat them aloud. • Discuss meaning of word. Use word in context.

Recognize Long Uu Vowel Teams Syllable Patterns (u, ew, ue)

Introduce

As students participate in this lesson, they will identify the name and sound of the target vowel patterns, and they will identify the letter or letters when the sound and name is given orally. Students will apply their knowledge by recognizing the medial sound of target sounds using pictures.

State Learning Goal

Say: *Today we will learn to read words with the long sound of vowel* **u** *using vowel teams. Vowel teams are when one or two vowels are put together to form one sound. We are going to read words with the vowel teams* **u, ew, ue**.

Teach

Say: *Letters represent sounds. We remember the sounds each letter makes. We use letters to write words we say. We use letters to read and write words. The letter* **u** *is a vowel. It has a long sound /ū/ and a short sound /u/. We are going to learn words that have the long sound of vowel* **u** *using the vowel teams* **u, ew,** *and* **ue**.

Phonemic Awareness

Show picture of sound/spelling card to review long sound of **u**.

Say: *Listen to this sound: /ū/. Say it with me: /ū/. Say it on your own: /ū/.*

Say: *This is the long sound of vowel /ū/. It sounds like it is saying its name: /ū/, say it again /ū/.*

Sound-Spelling Correspondence

Write the word **flute** on the board. Point out the vowel **u** in the middle of the word.

Say: *The word flute has the long /ū/ sound in the middle and is spelled using the letter* **u**.

Write the word **duel** on the board. Point out the vowel **u** in the middle of the word.

Say: *Look at the word* **duel**. *The word* **duel** *has the long /ū/ sound in the middle and is spelled using the vowel team* **ue**.

Model

Use BLM 7, Row 1.

Say: *Look at each picture. Say its name. Listen for the long sound of /ū/.*

Say: *Do you hear the long sound of /ū/ in the word flute? Point to the letters that form the long sound of /ū/ in the picture.*

Lesson Objectives

- Identify and name long **u** vowel teams syllable patterns **u, ew, ue**.
- Produce the sound of long **u** vowel teams syllable patterns **u, ew, ue**.
- Relate the long sound /ū/ to the syllable patterns **u, ew, ue**.
- Recognize long vowel sound /ū/ in words/pictures.
- Recognize long vowel team of syllable patterns with long **u**.

Metacognitive Strategy
- Selective Auditory Attention
- Imagery
- Auditory Representation

Academic Language
- letter name, letter sound, vowel, long vowel sound, syllable, vowel team, pattern

Additional Materials
- Sound Spelling Card **Uu**
- Blackline Master 7

Pre-Assess
Student's ability to recognize the long vowel sound represented by the target letter of the alphabet and to identify the letter used to represent the corresponding sound. Ability to pronounce the long vowel sound.

Practice

Use BLM 7, Row 2

Say: *Look at the picture. Say its name. Listen for the long sound of /ū/. Is it spelled with* **a u, ue,** *or* **ew?**

Say: *What is shown by the first picture? a* **duel** *Do you hear the long sound /ū/ in the word* **duel***? Point to the letters that form the long sound of /ū/ in each picture.*

Repeat with **dew.**

Apply

Blend Words

Use BLM 7, Row 3.

Say: *Look at each letter and listen to the long sound of vowel /ū/ as I read:* **/ch/ /ū/.** *Your turn:* **/ch/ /ū/.**

Say: *Now we are going to blend the sounds together by stretching them out as we read them.* Point to each letter in a sweeping motion left to right **/chūūū/.**

Ask: *What word?* **(chew)**.

Repeat with **suit** and **fuse.**

Spelling

Use BLM 7, Row 4.

Say: *Now we can practice writing the sounds we hear in each word. Call one word at a time, stretching each sound.*

Say: *Say the word slowly; write a letter for each sound you hear.*

Conclusion

Ask: *What did we learn today? We learned that the vowel* **u** *makes the long sound /ṳ/. We also learned that the vowel teams* **ue** *and* **ew** *make the long sound /ṳ/. What pictures/words will help you remember the long sound /ṳ/?*

Home Connection

Encourage students to practice identifying the long vowel sound **/u/** in words with a family member.

Formative Assessment

If the student completes each task correctly, proceed to the next skill in the sequence. If not, refer to suggested Intervention 2.

Did the student...?	Intervention 2
Identify the name of the letters?	• Use physical rhythmic movements as the letter name is repeated. March while chanting the letter name. Move arms up and down. Sway from side to side.
Identify the sounds of the letters?	• Use exaggeration of forming the /ū/ by opening the mouth wide and bringing the lips together in a pucker.
Produce the sounds of the letters?	• Use mirrors to show the movement of the mouth, tongue, and teeth as the sound is produced. Use hand over mouth to explore movement of air as the sound is produced
Recognize the CVC or CVCe pattern?	• Arrange a list of common same vowel words vertically, point out pattern.
Know the names of pictures?	• Tell students the names of pictures, have student repeat them aloud. • Discuss meaning of word. Use word in context.

Recognize R-controlled Syllable Patterns with Long Ee

Introduce

As students participate in this lesson, they will identify the name and sound of the target letter, and they will identify the letter when the sound and name is given orally. Students will apply their knowledge by recognizing the initial sound of the target letter using pictures.

State Learning Goal

Say: *Today we will learn to read words with the long sound of vowel* **e** *in r-controlled syllable patterns.*

Teach

Say: *Letters represent sounds. We remember the sounds each letter makes. We use letters to write words we say. We use letters to read and write words. The letter* **e** *is a vowel. It has a long sound /ē/ found in the syllables* **ear, eer** *and* **ere***. We are going to learn words that have the long sound of vowel* **e** *in the r-controlled syllables of* **ear, eer** *and* **ere***.

Phonemic Awareness

Show picture of sound/spelling card to review long sound of /ē/.

Say: *Listen to this sound /ē/. Say it with me: /ē/. Say it on your own: /ē/.*

Say: *This is the long sound of vowel* **e***. It sounds like it is saying its name: /ē/. Say it again, /ē/.*

Say: *We can also hear the long sound of vowel* **e** *in words with the letter patterns of* **ear, eer,** *and* **ere***. Some of these words can be homophones. Homophones are words that sound the same but are spelled differently and have different meanings, like* **hear** *and* **here.**

Sound-Spelling Correspondence

Show the letters.

Say: *We can write the long vowel sound /ē/ with the letter patterns of* **ear, eer,** *and* **ere***.*

Say: *We hear the sound /ē/ in the letter patterns of* **ear, eer,** *and* **ere***.*

Write the word **fear** on the board. Point out the vowel **e**.

Say: *When you see the vowel* **e** *in the syllable* **ear** *the vowel* **e** *makes its long sound.*

Write the word **cheer** on the board. Point out the vowel **e**.

Say: *When you see the vowel* **e** *in the syllable* **eer** *the vowel* **e** *makes its long sound.*

Write the word **here** on the board. Point out the vowel **e**.

Say: *When you see the vowel* **e** *in the syllables* **ere** *the vowel* **e** *makes its long sound.*

Lesson Objectives

- Identify the long vowel sound of **e** in r-controlled syllable patterns.
- Produce the sound of letter **e** in r-controlled syllable patterns.
- Relate the sound /ē/ to the letters **ear, eer, ere.**
- Recognize long vowel sound /ē/ in words/pictures.

Metacognitive Strategy
- Selective Auditory Attention
- Imagery
- Auditory Representation

Academic Language
- letter name, letter sound, vowel, long vowel sound, silent e, pattern

Additional Materials
- Sound Spelling Card Ee, Aa, Rr
- Blackline Master 8

Pre-Assess
Student's ability to recognize the long vowel sound represented by the target letter of the alphabet and to identify the letters used to represent the corresponding sound. Ability to pronounce the long vowel sound.

Model
Use BLM 8, Row 1.

Say: *Look at each picture. Say its name. Listen for the long sound /ē/. Does it have the syllable* **ear, eer,** *or* **ere***?*

Say: *Look at the first picture. Do you hear the long sound /ē/ in the word* **cheer?** *If we hear the sound /ē/ with the syllable* **ear, eer,** *or* **ere,** *we will circle the picture. If we do not hear the sound /ē/ in these syllables, we cross out the picture.*

Practice
Use BLM 8, Row 2.

Say: *Look at the picture. Say its name. Listen for the long sound of /ē/. Does the word hear have the syllable* **ear, eer,** *or* **ere***?*

Ask: *Do you hear the long sound /ē/ in* **ear***? Write the word.*

Apply
Blend Words
Use BLM 8, Row 3.

Say: *Look at each letter and listen to the long sound of vowel /e/ as I read /h/ /ē/ /r/. Your turn: /h/ /ē/ /r/.*

Say: *Now we are going to blend the sounds together by stretching them out as we read them.*

Point to each letter in a sweeping motion left to right **/hhhēēerrr/**.

Ask: *What word?* (**here**)

Spelling
Use BLM 8, Row 4.

Say: *Now we can practice writing the sounds we hear in each word. Call one word at a time, stretching each sound.*

Say: *Say the word slowly; write a letter for each sound you hear.*

Conclusion
Ask: *What did we learn today? We learned that the vowel* **e** *makes the long sound /ē/ in the r-controlled syllables of* **ear, eer,** *and* **ere***. What pictures/words will help you remember the long sound /ē/ with the syllables ear, eer, and ere?*

Home Connection
Encourage students to practice identifying the long vowel sound **e** in **ear**, **eer**, and **ere** syllable words with a family member.

 Formative Assessment

If the student completes each task correctly, proceed to the next skill in the sequence. If not, refer to suggested Intervention 2.

Did the student...?	Intervention 2
Identify the name of the letters?	• Use physical rhythmic movements as the letter name is repeated. March while chanting the letter name. Move arms up and down. Sway from side to side.
Identify the sounds of the letters?	• Say words with the target sounds by repeating the words three times. Examples: hear hear hear, here here here, cheer cheer cheer.
Produce the sounds of the letters?	• Use mirrors to show the movement of the mouth, tongue, and teeth as the sound is produced. Use hand over mouth to explore movement of air as the sound is produced
Recognize the CVCe pattern?	• Arrange a list of common same vowel CVCe words vertically, and point out the pattern.
Know the names of pictures?	• Tell students the names of pictures, have student repeat them aloud. • Discuss meaning of word. Use word in context.

Recognize R-controlled Syllable Patterns with Long Aa

Introduce

As students participate in this lesson, they will identify the name and sound of the target letter, and they will identify the letter when the sound and name is given orally. Students will apply their knowledge by recognizing the initial sound of target letter using pictures.

State Learning Goal

Say: *Today we will learn to read words with the long sound of vowel **a** in r-controlled syllable patterns.* .

Teach

Say: *Letters represent sounds. We remember the sounds each letter makes. We use letters to write words we say. We use letters to read and write words. The letter **a** is a vowel. It has a long sound /ā/ found in the syllables **air** and **are**. We are going to learn words that have the long sound of vowel **a** in the r-controlled syllables of **air** and **are**.*

Phonemic Awareness

Show picture of sound/spelling card to review **long sound of Aa**

Say: *Listen to this sound /ā/. Say it with me: /ā/. Say it on your own: /ā/.*

Say: *This is the long sound of vowel **a**. It sounds like it is saying its name: /ā/. Say it again, /ā/.*

Say: *We can also hear the long sound of vowel **a** in words with the letter patterns of **air** and **are**. Some of these words can be homophones. Homophones are words that sound the same but are spelled differently and have different meanings, like **fair** and **fare**.*

Sound-Spelling Correspondence

Show the letters.

Say: *We can write the long vowel sound /ā/ with the letter patterns of **air** and **are**.*

Say: *We hear the sound /ā/ in the letter patterns of **air** and **are**.*

Write the word **fair** on the board. Point out the vowel **a**.

Say: *When you see the vowel **a** in the syllable **air** the vowel **a** makes its long sound.*

Write the word **fare** on the board. Point out the vowel **a**.

Say: *When you see the vowel **a** in the syllable **are** the vowel **a** makes its long sound.*

Lesson Objectives

- Identify the long vowel sound /ā/ in r-controlled syllable patterns.
- Produce the sound of letter **a** in r-controlled syllable patterns.
- Relate the sound /ā/ to the words air, are.
- Recognize long vowel sound /ā/ in words/pictures.

Metacognitive Strategy
- Selective Auditory Attention
- Imagery
- Auditory Representation

Academic Language
- letter name, letter sound, vowel, long vowel sound, silent e, pattern

Additional Materials
- Sound Spelling Card **Ee, Aa, Ii, Rr**
- Blackline Master 9

Pre-Assess

Student's ability to recognize the long vowel sound represented by the target letter of the alphabet and to identify the letters used to represent the corresponding sound. Ability to pronounce the long vowel sound.

Model

Use BLM 9, Row 1

Say: *Look at each picture. Say its name. Listen for the long sound of /ā/. Does it have the syllable **air** or **are**?*

Say: *Look at the first picture. Do you hear the long sound of /ā/ in the word **chair**? If we hear the sound of /ā/ with the syllable **air** or **are**, we will circle the picture. If we do not hear the sound /ā/ in these syllables, we will cross out the picture.*

Practice

Use BLM 9, Row 2

Say: *Look at the first picture. Say its name. Listen for the long sound of /ā/. Does the word **fair** have the syllable **air** or **are**?*

Say: *Do you hear the long sound /ā/? If so, write the word.*

Apply

Blend Words

Use BLM 9, Row 3

Say: *Look at each letter and listen to the long sound of vowel a as I read: /f/ /ā/ /r/. Your turn: /f/ /ā/ /r/.*

Say: *Now we are going to blend the sounds together by stretching them out as we read them.*

Point to each letter in a sweeping motion left to right **/fffaaarrr/**.

Ask: *What word?* **(fare)**

Spelling

Use BLM 9, Row 4.

Say: *Now we can practice writing the sounds we hear in each word. Call one word at a time, stretching each sound.*

Say: *Say the word slowly; write a letter for each sound you hear.*

Conclusion

Ask: *What did we learn today? We learned that the vowel **a** makes the long sound /a/ in the r-controlled syllables of air and are. What pictures/words will help you remember the long sound /a/ with the syllables air and are?*

Home Connection

Encourage students to practice identifying the long vowel sound **/a/** in air and are syllable words with a family member.

✔ Formative Assessment

If the student completes each task correctly, proceed to the next skill in the sequence. If not, refer to the suggested Intervention 2.

Did the student...?	Intervention 2
Identify the name of the letters?	• Use physical rhythmic movements as the letter name is repeated. March while chanting the letter name. Move arms up and down. Sway from side to side.
Identify the sounds of the letters?	• Say words with the target sounds by repeating the words three times. Examples: fair fair fair, mare mare mare.
Produce the sounds of the letters?	• Use mirrors to show the movement of the mouth, tongue, and teeth as the sound is produced. Use hand over mouth to explore movement of air as the sound is produced
Recognize the CVCe pattern?	• Arrange a list of common same vowel CVCe words vertically, point out pattern.
Know the names of pictures?	• Tell students the names of pictures, have student repeat them aloud. • Discuss meaning of word. Use word in context.

Recognize Vowel-C-e Syllable Pattern

Lesson Objectives

- Identify and name words with the long vowel VCe pattern.
- Produce the sound of words with the long vowel VCe pattern.
- Relate the long vowel sounds to their letters
- Recognize long vowel sounds in words/pictures with the VCe pattern.
- Recognize long vowel sound (VCe) pattern in VCe words.

Metacognitive Strategy
- Selective Auditory Attention
- Imagery
- Auditory Representation

Academic Language
- letter name, letter sound, vowel, long vowel sound, silent e, pattern

Additional Materials
- Sound Spelling Cards **e, a, i, o, u**
- Blackline Master 10

Pre-Assess
Student's ability to recognize the short vowel sound represented by the target letter of the alphabet and to identify the letter used to represent the corresponding sound. Ability to pronounce the long vowel sound.

Introduce

As students participate in this lesson, they will identify the name and sound of the target letter, and they will identify the letter when the sound and name is given orally. Students will apply their knowledge by recognizing the initial sound of the target letter using pictures.

State Learning Goal

Say: *Today we will learn to read words with long vowel sounds. We are going to learn that when we put the vowel* **e** *at the end of some words, the first vowel in the word makes its long sound and the vowel* **e** *is a silent* **e**.

Teach

Say: *Letters represent sounds. We remember the sounds each letter makes. We use letters to write words we say. We use letters to read and write words. The letter* **e** *is a vowel. It has a long sound /ē/ and a short sound /e/. We are going to learn words that have the long sound of vowel* **e**. *We will repeat with the letters* **a, i, o,** *and* **u**.

Phonemic Awareness

Show picture of sound/spelling card to review long sound of **e**.

Say: *Listen to this sound /ē/. Say it with me: /ē/. Say it on your own: /ē/.*

Say: *This is the long sound of vowel* **e**. *It sounds like it is saying its name: /ē/, say it again /ē/.*

Repeat with the letters **a, i, o,** and **u**.

Sound-Spelling Correspondence

Write the word **eve** on the board. Point out the vowel **e** at the beginning of the word and the vowel **e** at the end.

Say: *when you see vowel* **e** *at the end of a four-letter word, the* **e** *is silent and the first vowel makes its long sound.*

Say: *Look at the word* **eve**. *Does it have a vowel* **e** *at the end? Then vowel* **e** *says its name.*

Say: *Read it with me:* **eve**.

Repeat with the words **bake**, **bike**, **rose**, **cube**.

Model

Use BLM 10, Row 1.

Explain that some two-syllable words have one syllable with the vowel-consonant-e pattern that students have been learning in words such as **bike** and **five**. For example, **inside** has two syllables. Remind students that each syllable has a vowel sound.

Say: *We divide the word between the two consonants: in side. The first syllable is closed and has a short vowel sound. A syllable with the vowel-consonant-e usually has a long vowel sound. The syllable side has the vowel-consonant-e pattern, and so the vowel sound is long* **i: side**. *Look at the pictures. If you hear the long* **i** *sound, circle the picture. If you don't hear the long* **i** *sound, cross out the picture.*

Practice
Use BLM 10, Row 2.

Display the words. Have students divide each word into syllables, tell the vowel sound in each syllable, and then blend the syllables to read the word: **reptile, invite, landscape**.

Apply
Blend Words
Use BLM 10, Row 3.

Say: *Look at each letter and listen to the long sound of vowel* **i** *as I read:* /r/ /e/ /p/ /t/ /ī/ /l/. *Your turn:* /r/ /e/ /p/ /t/ /ī/ /l/.

Say: *Now we are going to blend the sounds together by stretching them out as we read them.* Point to each letter in a sweeping motion left to right /reeeptīīīlll/.

Ask: *What is the word?* (**reptile**)

Repeat with the words **invade** and **landscape**.

Spelling
Use BLM 10, Row 4.

Say: *Now we can practice writing the sounds we hear in each word. Call one word at a time, stretching each sound.*

Say: *Say the word slowly; write a letter for each sound you hear.*

Conclusion
Ask: *What did we learn today? We learned that words with the vowel-consonant-silent e pattern makes long vowel sounds when vowel* **e** *is at the end. What pictures/words will help you remember long vowel sounds with the silent* **e** *at the end?*

Home Connection

Encourage students to practice identifying the long vowel sounds in VCe words with a family member.

✔ **Formative Assessment**

If the student completes each task correctly, proceed to the next skill in the sequence. If not, refer to the suggested Intervention 2.

Did the student...?	Intervention 2
Identify the name of the letters?	• Use physical rhythmic movements as the letter name is repeated. March while chanting the letter name. Move arms up and down. Sway from side to side.
Identify the sounds of the letters?	• Use exaggeration when forming the long vowel sounds with your mouth.
Produce the sounds of the letters?	• Use mirrors to show the movement of the mouth, tongue, and teeth as the sound is produced. Use hand over mouth to explore movement of air as the sound is produced
Recognize the VCe pattern?	• Arrange a list of common same vowel VCe words vertically, point out pattern.
Know the names of pictures?	• Tell students the names of pictures, have students repeat them aloud. • Discuss meaning of word. Use word in context.

Identify and Name LE Syllables

Introduce

As students participate in this lesson, they will identify the name and sound of the targeted letters, and they will identify the letters when the sounds and names are given orally. Students will apply their knowledge by recognizing the sounds of target endings using pictures.

State Learning Goal

Say: *Today we will practice listening to the sound /le/ that the letters le make to form the final syllable in two-syllable words.*

Teach

Say: *Letters represent sounds. We remember the sounds each letter makes. We use letters to write words we say. We use letters to read and write words. Letters are made up of vowels and consonants. Each vowel sound in a word is a syllable.*

Phonemic Awareness

Show letter cards **l** and **e** to review the sound.

Say: *Listen to this sound: /le/. Say it with me: /le/. Say it on your own: /le/.*

Sound-Spelling Correspondence

Show the letters.

Say: *The way we write the sound /le/ is with the letters le.*

Say: *The letters le makes the sound /le/.*

Say: *The letters le make a syllable when /le/ is the final sound in a word.*

Ask: *What is the name of the letters? (le) What sound does the letters make? /le/*

Model

Use BLM 11, Row 1.

Say: *We will look at each picture and say its name. If we hear the sound of the syllable le at the end of the word, we will circle the letters le. If we do not hear the sound of the syllable /le/ at the end of the word, we cross out the picture.*

Say: *What do you see in the first picture? (a circle) Do you hear the sound of the syllable /le/ at the end of the word circle? Circle the letters le. If you do not hear the sound of the syllable /le/ at the end of the word, then cross out the picture.*

Lesson Objectives

- Identify and name the letters **le.**
- Produce the sound of word ending **le.**
- Relate the sound /**le**/ to the letters **le.**
- Recognize the sound /**le**/ in words/pictures.

Metacognitive Strategy
- Selective Auditory Attention
- Imagery
- Auditory Representation

Academic Language
- letter name, letter sound, final sound, ending sound

Additional Materials
- Letter Cards **l, e**
- Blackline Master 11

Pre-Assess
Student's ability to recognize the sounds represented by the targeted letters of the alphabet and to identify the letters used to represent the corresponding sounds.

Practice

Use BLM 11, Row 2

Say: *Look at the picture. Say its name. Write the letters.*

Say: *What does the first picture show?* **(cattle)** *Do you hear the sound of the syllable /le/ at the end of the word* **cattle***? Write the letters* **le***.*

Apply

Blend Words

Use BLM 11, Row 3.

Say: *Look at each letter and listen to the sound as I read: /t/ /ûr/ /t/ /l/. Your turn: /t/ /ûr/ /t/ /l/.*

Say: *Now we are going to blend the sounds together by stretching them out as we read them.*

Point to each letter in a sweeping motion left to right **/tûrtlll/.**

Ask: *What word?* **(turtle)**

Repeat for other words

Spelling

Use BLM 11, Row 4.

Say: *Now we can practice writing the sounds we hear in each word.* **Call one word at a time, stretching each sound.**

Say: *Say the word slowly; write a letter for each sound you hear.*

Conclusion

Ask: *What did we learn today? We learned that the letters* **le** *makes the sound /le/. We learned to listen for the sound of this syllable at the end of words. We wrote words using the letters* **le** *at the end of words. What pictures/words will help you remember the sound /le/ and the letters* **le** *at the end of a word?*

Home Connection

Encourage students to practice identifying sound **le** at the end of words and writing the letters **le** with a family member. Encourage students to identify other words with the sound of syllable **le** at the end of words with their family.

✔ Formative Assessment

If the student completes each task correctly, proceed to the next skill in the sequence. If not, refer to the suggested Intervention 2.

Did the student…?	Intervention 2
Identify the names of the letters?	• Use physical rhythmic movements as the letter name is repeated. March while chanting the letter name. Move arms up and down. Sway from side to side.
Identify the sound of the letters?	• Say words with the target sounds by clearly separating the syllables in the words. Examples: tur/tle, cir/cle, mar/ble.
Produce the sound of the letters?	• Use mirrors to show the movement of the mouth, tongue, and teeth as the sound is produced. • Use hand over mouth to explore movement of air as the sound is produced.
Recognize the sounds of the consonant digraphs?	• Use Elkonin boxes – student moves a token into the box as the sound of the consonant digraph is said in the word.
Write the letters?	• Write the letters, have students trace them. Create the letters with clay. Discuss letter features (lines, shape). Trace over the letters with multiple colors.
Know the names of pictures?	• Tell students the names of pictures, have students repeat them aloud. Discuss word and use each word in context.

Decode Words with Common Suffixes: -ar, -er, -or

Introduce

As students participate in this lesson, they will understand that suffixes are a group of letters added at the end of a root word to create a new word with a new meaning. Students will recognize and generalize the understanding that suffixes **-ar**, **-er**, and **-or** mean "one who."

State Learning Goal

Say: *Today we will practice adding the suffix **-ar**, **-er**, and **-or** to the end of a word to recognize how they change its meaning. We can use the suffixes **-ar**, **-er**, and **-or** as clues to figure out the meaning of a word.*

Teach

Say: *A suffix is a group of letters that can be added to the end of a word.*

Ask: *To what part of a word is the suffix added? A suffix is added to the end of a word. Write the word teach on the board. Write the suffix **-er** on the board.*

Say: *This is the word **teach**. Read it with me: **teach**. This is the suffix **-er**. Read it with me: **-er**. I will add the suffix **-er** at the end of the word teach to make the word **teacher**. **Teacher** means "one who teaches." The meaning of the word **teach** changed.*

Write the word sail on the board. Write the suffix **-or** on the board.

Say: *This is the word **sail**. Read it with me: **sail**. This is the suffix **-or**. Read it with me: **-or**. I will add the suffix **-or** at the end of the word **sail** to make the word sailor. **Sailor** means "one who sails." The meaning of the word **sail** changed.*

Say: *When you add a suffix to the end of a word, it changes the meaning of the word.*

Ask: *What happens when you add a suffix to the end of a word? The meaning of the word changes.*

Model

Use BLM 12, Row 1.

Say: *Look at the first picture. I read the word **sing**. I add **-er**. It reads: **singer**. It means "one who sings." You can use the suffixes **-er**, **-or** and the suffix **-ar** to understand the meaning of a word.*

Lesson Objectives

- Recognize and decode common suffixes.
- Recognize that suffixes placed at the end of a root/base word change the meaning of the word.

Metacognitive Strategy
- Selective Auditory Attention
- Use Deductive Thinking
- Generalize a Rule

Academic Language
- word ending, different meaning, suffix, base word, root word
- Note: When using Latin-based suffixes, the base word is called a root word.

Additional Materials
- Blackline Master 12

Pre-Assess
Student's ability to recognize the end of a word as a clue to word meaning
Student's ability to recognize a base or root word as the part of the word that contains meaning and can stand alone.

Practice

Use BLM 12, Row 2

Say: *Look at the first picture. Let's read the word* **collect**. *Let's add* **-or**. *It reads:* **collector**. *It means "one who collects." Let's read the word* **paint**. *Let's add* **-er**. *It reads:* **painter**. *It means "one who paints." You can use the suffixes* **-er**, **-or**, **-ar** *to understand the meaning of a word.*

Apply

Blend Words

Use BLM 12, Row 3

Say: *You read the word* **act**. *You add* **-or**. *It reads:* **actor**. *What does it mean? You can use the suffix* **-er** *or suffix* **-or** *to understand the meaning of a word.*

Spelling

Use BLM 12, Row 4.

Say: *Now we can practice writing the sounds we hear in each word.* **Call one word at a time, stretching each sound.**

Say: *Say the word slowly; write a letter for each sound you hear.*

Conclusion

Ask: *What did we learn today? We learned that when we add the suffix* **-er**, *the suffix* **-or** *or the suffix* **-ar** *to the end of a word, it changes the meaning of the word. The suffixes* **-er**, **-or**, *and* **-ar** *all mean "one who."*

Home Connection

Ask students to practice adding **-er, -ar**, and **-or** to the end of words and to understand the meaning of the new word created. Have students identify other words that have the suffix **-er, -or**, or **-ar** with a family member.

✔ **Formative Assessment**

If the student completes each task correctly, proceed to the next skill in the sequence. If not, refer to suggested intervention 2.

Did the student…?	Intervention 2
Recognize and identify the end of a word?	• Point directly to the end of the word. Say this is the end of the word____ or the last part of the word____. Point to the beginning and say, this is the beginning or the first part of the word
Repeat words and phrases when asked?	• Point to the word and have students echo-read, then read it on their own while pointing to the word

Identify and Decode Suffixes: -y, -ly

Introduce

As students participate in this lesson, they will identify **-y** and **-ly** suffixes and understand how they change the meaning of words. Students will apply their knowledge by recognizing target suffixes using pictures and words and adding them to root words using the correct spelling rules.

State Learning Goal

Say: *Today we will practice identifying and writing words that end in -y and -ly and understand how they change the meanings of words.*

Teach

Say: *We add a* **-y** *to a noun to form an adjective or describing word. For example, we add* **-y** *to the noun* **mist** *to get the adjective* **misty.** *"It is a misty day."*

We add an **-ly** *to turn adjectives into adverbs, words that tell how something is done. For example the adjective* **quiet** *becomes the adverb* **quietly.** *"He spoke quietly."*

Phonemic Awareness

Display the word **bumpy** and point to the **y**.

Say: *the letter* **-y** *at the end has the* /ē/ *sound. Say it with me:* /ē/. *Say it on your own:* /ē/.

Then display the word **quickly** and point to the suffix **-ly**.

Say: *The* **-ly** *ending has this sound* /lē/. *Say it with me:* /lē/. *Say it on your own:* /lē/.

Sound-Spelling Correspondence

Show the letter.

Say: *We can write the sound* /ē/ *at the end of a word with the letter* **y.**

Say: *The letter* **y** *makes the sound* /ē/. *We add the letter* **y** *to the end of a noun to make an adjective.*

Ask: *What is the name of the letter?* (**y**) *What sound does the letter make?* (/ē/)

Say: *We can write the sound* /lē/ *at the end of a word with the letters* **ly.**

Say: *The letters* **ly** *makes the sound* /lē/. *We add the letters* **ly** *to the end of a noun to make an adverb.*

Ask: *What are the names of the letters?* (**l** *and* **y**) *What sounds do the letters make?* /lē/

Lesson Objectives

- Identify and name the **-y** and **-ly** suffixes.
- Understand that adding **-y** and **-ly** to words changes their meaning.
- Understand the spelling rules for adding the suffixes **-y** and **-ly** to root words.

Metacognitive Strategy
- Selective Auditory Attention
- Imagery
- Auditory Representation

Academic Language
- final sound, ending sound, suffix, adjective, adverb

Additional Materials
- Sound/Spelling Cards: **-y** and **-ly** endings
- Blackline Master 13

Pre-Assess
Student's ability to recognize root words and suffixes

Model

Use BLM 13, Row 1.

Say: *Look at the pictures. Name the types of weather.*

Ask: *What do you see in the first picture?* (**rain**) *What kind of day does this picture show? It is a rainy day. Write the adjective **rainy** under the picture.*

Repeat with the other two words.

Practice

Use BLM 13, Row 2.

Say: *Look at the words. Add the suffix -**ly** to change the words into adverbs. Let's say the first word **angry**.*

Ask: *What do I need to do to the word **angry** before I add -**ly**? Change the **y** to **i**, angrily.*

Apply

Blend Words

Use BLM 13, Row 3.

Say: *Look at each letter and listen to the sound as I read: /s/ /p/ /o/ /t/ /ē/. Your turn: /s/ /p/ /o/ /t/ /ē/.*

Say: *Now we are going to blend the sounds together by stretching them out as we read them.* Point to each letter in a sweeping motion left to right. **/ssspoteēē/**

Ask: *What word?* (**spotty**)

Repeat with the other two words.

Spelling

Use BLM 13, Row 4.

Say: *Now we can practice writing the sounds we hear in each word. Call one word at a time, stretching each sound.*

Say: *Say the word slowly; write a letter for each sound you hear.*

Conclusion

Ask: *What did we learn today? We learned the suffix -**y** changes a noun to an adjective and the suffix -**ly** changes a word to an adverb. We also learned the special spelling rules for adding these suffixes correctly.*

Home Connection

Encourage students to practice identifying adjectives and adverbs with a family member. Encourage students to identify other words that end with **y** and **ly** with their family and to explain the rules for their spelling.

✔ Formative Assessment

If the student completes each task correctly, proceed to the next skill in the sequence. If not, refer to the suggested Intervention 2.

Did the student…?	Intervention 2
Identify the name of the letter?	• Use physical rhythmic movements as the letter name is repeated. March while chanting the letter name. Move arms up and down. Sway from side to side.
Identify the sound of the letter?	• Say words with the target suffixes **y** and **ly**, emphasizing the sound eee/ leee: bad lee bump eee
Produce the sound of the letter?	• Use mirrors to show the movement of the mouth, tongue, and teeth as the sound is produced. Use hand over mouth to explore movement of air as the sound is produced
Recognize the final sounds?	• Use Elkonin boxes – student moves a token into the last box as the final sound of the word is said.
Write the letter?	• Write the letter, have students trace it. Create the letter with clay. • Discuss letter features (lines, shape). Trace over the letter with multiple colors.
Know the name of pictures?	• Tell students the name of pictures, have students repeat them aloud. Discuss word and use each word in context.

Decode Words with Common Prefixes: re-

Introduce

As students participate in this lesson, they will understand that prefixes are a group of letters added at the beginning of a word to create a new word with a new meaning. Students will recognize and generalize the understanding that the prefix **re-** means "again, to do again."

State Learning Goal

Say: *Today we will practice adding the prefix* **re-** *to the beginning of a verb or action word to recognize how it changes its meaning. We will learn we can use the prefix* **re-** *as a clue to figure out the meaning of a word.*

Teach

Say: *A prefix is a group of letters that can be added to the beginning of a word.*

Ask: *To what part of a word is the prefix added? A prefix is added to the beginning of a word.*

Write the word **do** on the board. Write the prefix **re-** on the board.

Say: *This is the word* **do**. *Read it with me:* **do**. *This is the prefix* **re-**. *Read it with me* **re-**. *I will add the prefix* **re-** *at the beginning of the word do to make the word* **redo**. **Redo** *means "do again." For instance, we say, we need to* **redo** *the work we did yesterday. The prefix* **re-** *changed the meaning of the word, and created a new word* **redo** *that means "do again."*

Write the word **count** on the board again. Write the prefix **re-** on the board.

Say: *This is the word* **count**. *Read it with me:* **count**. *This is the prefix* **re-**. *Read it with me:* **re-**. *I will add the prefix* **re-** *at the beginning of the word* **count** *to make the word* **recount**. **Recount** *means "count again." For example, we say, "Let's recount the candles on the cake to make sure we have six." The prefix* **re-** *changed the meaning of the word* **count** *to mean "count again."*

Model

Use BLM 14, Row 1.

Say: *I read the word* **name**. *I add* **re-**. *It reads:* **rename**. *It means "name again." You can use the prefix* **re-** *to understand the meaning of an action word or verb, because the prefix* **re-** *means to "repeat the action" or to "do the action again."*

Lesson Objectives

- Recognize and decode common prefixes.
- Recognize that prefixes are placed at the beginning of a root/base word change the meaning of the word.

Metacognitive Strategy
- Selective Auditory Attention
- Use Deductive Thinking
- Generalize a Rule

Academic Language
- word ending, different meaning, prefix, base word, root word.
- Note: When using Latin-based suffixes, the base word is called a root word.

Additional Materials
- Blackline Master 14

Pre-Assess

Student's ability to recognize the beginning of a word as a clue to word meaning. Student's ability to recognize a base or root word as the part of the word that contains meaning and can stand alone.

Practice

Use BLM 14, Row 2–4.

Say: *Let's read the word* **write**. *Let's add* **re-**. *It reads:* **rewrite**. *It means to "write again." Remember, you can use the prefix* **re-** *to understand the meaning of an action word or verb, because the prefix* **re-** *means to "do again."*

Repeat the procedure with **fresh** and **visit**.

Apply

Blend Words

Use BLM 14, Row 5–7.

Say: *You read the word* **open**. *Add* **re-** *at the beginning of the word. It reads:* **reopen**. *What does it mean? It means "open again." You can use the prefix* **re-** *to understand the meaning of an action or verb because the prefix* **re-** *means to "do again."*

Repeat the procedure with **state** and **load**.

Conclusion

Ask: *What did we learn today? We learned that when we add the prefix* **re–** *at the beginning of an action word or verb, it creates a new word that means repeating the action or doing it again.*

Home Connection

Ask students to practice adding the prefix **re-** to the beginning of action words or verbs to understand the meaning of the new word created. Have students identify action words or verbs to which the prefix **re-** can be added to create a new word with a family member.

✔ Formative Assessment

If the student completes each task correctly, proceed to the next skill in the sequence. If not, refer to suggested intervention 2.

Did the student…?	Intervention 2
Recognize and identify the beginning or end of a word?	• Point directly to the beginning and say, this is the beginning or the first part of the word ____. Point directly to the end of the word and say this is the end of the word____ or the last part of the word____. Say and point: Show me the beginning of the word. Show me the end of the word.
Understand the meaning of **re-** is "do something again?"	• Say that to do something again means 'to repeat the action." Then dramatize an action. • Say: Write, I write on a piece of paper. Then write again. • Say: I rewrite on a piece of paper. • Act out: open/reopen, try/retry, name/rename, arrange/rearrange.
Read words?	• Point to each word and have students repeat, echo, then read it on their own while pointing to the word. Use the word in short sentences and explain its meaning to ensure student understanding.

Decode Words with Common Prefixes: un-, non-

Introduce

As students participate in this lesson, they will understand that prefixes are a group of letters added at the beginning of a word to create a new word with a new meaning. Students will recognize and generalize the understanding that the prefixes **un-** and **non-** mean "not."

State Learning Goal

Say: *Today we will practice adding the prefix **un-** or **non-** to the beginning of a word to recognize how it changes its meaning. We will learn we can use the prefixes un- and non- as a clue to figure out the meaning of a word.*

Teach

Say: *A prefix is a group of letters that can be added to the beginning of a word.*

Ask: *To what part of a word is the prefix added? A prefix is added to the beginning of a word.*

Write the word **able** on the board. Write the prefix **un-** on the board.

Say: *This is the word able. Read it with me: **able**. This is the prefix **un-**. Read it with me **un-**. I will add the prefix **un-** at the beginning of the word able to make the word **unable**. Unable means "not able." For instance, we say, "We are **unable** to go swimming." The prefix **un-** changed the meaning of the word and created a new word **unable** that means "not able."*

Write the word **fiction** on the board. Write the prefix **non-** on the board.

Ask: *This is the word **fiction**. Read it with me: **fiction**. This is the prefix **non-**. Read it with me: **non-**. I will add the prefix **non-** at the beginning of the word **fiction** to make the word **nonfiction**. Nonfiction means "not fiction." For example, we say, "The book is nonfiction." The prefix **non-** changed the meaning of the word **fiction**, and created a new word, **nonfiction**, which means "not fiction."*

Model

Use BLM 15, Row 1.

Say: *I read the word **lock**. I add **un-**. It reads: **unlock**. It means "not lock." You can use the prefix **un-** to understand the meaning of a word because the prefix **un-** means "not".*

Lesson Objectives

- Recognize and decode common prefixes.
- Recognize that prefixes are placed at the beginning of a root/base word change the meaning of the word.

Metacognitive Strategy
- Selective Auditory Attention
- Use Deductive Thinking
- Generalize a Rule

Academic Language
- word ending, different meaning, prefix, base word, root word.
- Note: When using Latin-based suffixes the base word is called a root word.

Additional Materials
- Blackline Master 15

Pre-Assess
Student's ability to recognize the beginning of a word as a clue to word meaning. Student's ability to recognize a base or root word as the part of the word that contains meaning and can stand alone.

Practice

Use BLM 15, Row 2–4.

Say: *Let's read the word* **able**. *Let's add* **un-**. *It reads:* **unable**. *It means "not able."* *Remember, you can use the prefixes* **non-** *or* **un-** *to understand the meaning of a word because the prefixes* **non-** *and* **un-** *mean to* "**not**."

Repeat the procedure with **aware** and **stop**.

Apply

Use BLM 15, Row 5–7.

Say: *You read the word* **available**. *Add* **un-** *at the beginning of the word. It reads:* **unavailable**. *What does it mean? It means "not available." You can use the prefix* **un-** *to understand the meaning word because the prefix* **un-** *means to "not."*

Repeat the procedure with **tie** and **sense**.

Conclusion

Ask: *What did we learn today? We learned that when we add the prefixes* **un–** *or* **non-** *at the beginning of a word, it creates a new word that means* **not**.

✔ Formative Assessment

If the student completes each task correctly, proceed to the next skill in the sequence. If not, refer to suggested intervention 2.

Did the student...?	Intervention 2
Recognize and identify the beginning or end of a word?	• Point directly to the beginning and say, this is the beginning or the first part of the word ___. Point directly to the end of the word and say this is the end of the word___ or the last part of the word___. Say and point: Show me the beginning of the word. Show me the end of the word.
Read words?	• Point to each word and have students repeat, echo, then read it on their own while pointing to the word. Use the word in short sentences and explain its meaning to ensure student understanding.

Decode Words with Common Suffixes: -ful, -less

Introduce

As students participate in this lesson, they will understand that suffixes are a group of letters added at the end of a root word to create a new word with a new meaning. Students will recognize and generalize the understanding that the suffix **-ful** means "full of, being, having." Students will recognize and generalize the understanding that the suffix **–less** means "not having, without."

State Learning Goal

Say: *Today we will practice adding the suffix **–ful** and the suffix **–less** to the end of a word to recognize how they change its meaning. We can use the suffix **–ful** and the suffix **–less** as clues to figure out the meaning of a word.*

Teach

Say: *A suffix is a group of letters that can be added to the end of a word.*

Ask: *To what part of a word is the suffix added? A suffix is added to the end of a word.*

Write the word **color** on the board. Write the suffix **–ful** on the board.

Say: *This is the word **color**. Read it with me: **color**. This is the suffix **-ful**. Read it with me **-ful**. I will add the suffix **–ful** at the end of the word **color** to make the word **colorful**. **Colorful** means "full of color." The meaning of the word **color** changed.*

Write the word **color** on the board again. Write the suffix **–less** on the board.

Say: *This is the suffix **-less**. Read it with me: **–less**. I will add the suffix **–less** at the end of the word color to make the word **colorless**. The word, **colorless** means "not having color, without color." The meaning of the word **color** changed.*

Model

Use BLM 16, Row 1.

Say: *I read the word **harm**. I add –**ful**. It reads: **harmful**. It means "full of harm." I read the word **harm** and add –**less**. It reads: **harmless**. It means "not having harm." You can use the suffix –**ful** and suffix –**less** to understand the meaning of a word.*

Lesson Objectives

- Recognize and decode common suffixes.
- Recognize that suffixes placed at the end of a root/base word change the meaning of the word.

Metacognitive Strategy
- Selective Auditory Attention
- Use Deductive Thinking
- Generalize a Rule

Academic Language
- word ending, different meaning, suffix, base word, root word.
- Note: When using Latin-based suffixes, the base word is called a root word.

Additional Materials
- Blackline Master 16

Pre-Assess
Student's ability to recognize the end of a word as a clue to word meaning
Student's ability to recognize a base or root word as the part of the word that contains meaning and can stand alone.

Practice

Use BLM 16, Row 2–4.

Say: *Let's read the word **law**. Let's add –**ful**. It reads: **lawful**. It means "full of law," or caring and obeying the law. Let's read the word **law**. Let's add –**less**. It reads: **lawless**. It means "not having law," or not obeying the law You can use the suffix –**ful** and suffix –**less** to understand the meaning of a word.*

Repeat the procedure with **care** and **mercy**.

Apply

Use BLM 16, Row 5–7.

Say: *Add –**ful** or –**less** to each of these words. Read each complete word. How did each suffix change the meaning of the word?*

Conclusion

Ask: *What did we learn today? We learned that when we add the suffix –**ful** or the suffix –**less** to the end of a word, it changes the meaning of the word. The suffix –**ful** means "full." The suffix –**less** means "not having" or "without."*

Home Connection

Ask students to practice adding –**ful** and –**less** to the end of words and to understand the meaning of the new word created. Have students identify other words that have the suffix –**ful** or –**less** with a family member.

✔ Formative Assessment

If the student completes each task correctly, proceed to the next skill in the sequence. If not, refer to suggested intervention 2.

Did the student...?	Intervention 2
Recognize and identify the end of a word?	• Point directly to the end of the word. Say this is the end of the word____ or the last part of the word____. Point to the beginning and say, this is the beginning or the first part of the word
Understand the meaning of –**ful** and –**less**?	• Show –**ful** and –**less** as opposite categories. Have students sort words under –**ful** and –**less** as the meaning of each pair of opposites are discussed: (colorful-colorless; joyful-joyless; careful-careless; restful-restless; hopeful-hopeless, flavorful-flavorless).
Repeat words and phrases when asked?	• Point to the word and have students echo-read, then read it on their own while pointing to the word

Decode Words with Common Suffixes: -like, -ish

Introduce

As students participate in this lesson, they will understand that affixes are a group of letters added at the beginning or end of a word to create a new word with a new meaning. Students will recognize that adjectives are words that are used to describe.

State Learning Goal

Say: *Today we will practice adding word parts to the end of words and recognize how it changes its meaning. We will learn we can use the word parts* **–like**, *and* **-ish** *as a clue to figure out the meaning of a word.*

Teach

Say: *A suffix is a group of letters that can be added to the end of a word.*

Ask: *To what part of a word is the suffix added? A suffix is added to the end of a word.*

Write the word **child** on the board. Write the suffix **like** on the board.

Say: *This is the word* **child**. *Read it with me:* **child**. *This is the suffix* **–like**. *Read it with me* **-like**. *I will add the suffix* **–like** *at the end of the word do to make the word* **childlike**. *The word* **childlike** *means "to act like a child." For instance, we say, "The way the dog plays is very childlike." The suffix* **–like** *changed the meaning of the word, and created a new word* **childlike** *that means "to act like a child."*

Write the word **child** on the board again. Write the suffix **–ish** on the board.

Say: *I will add the suffix* **–ish** *at the end of the word* **child** *to make the word* **childish**. *The word* **childish** *means "to act like a child," also. For example, we say, "Her behavior is very childish."*

Model

Use BLM 17, Row 1.

Say: *I read the word* **home**. *I add* **-like**. *It reads:* **homelike**. *It means "to resemble, or be like home." You can use the suffix* **–like** *to understand the meaning of a word because the suffix* **–like** *means "to resemble." Write the suffix to create the new word. Then write the new word.*

Lesson Objectives

- Recognize and decode common suffixes.
- Recognize that suffixes placed at the end of a root/base word change the meaning of the word.

Metacognitive Strategy
- Selective Auditory Attention
- Use Deductive Thinking
- Generalize a Rule

Academic Language
- word ending, different meaning, suffix, base word, root word, adjective, describe.
- Note: When using Latin-based suffixes the base word is called a root word.

Additional Materials
- Blackline Master 17

Pre-Assess

Student's ability to recognize a base or root word as the part of the word that contains meaning and can stand alone. Student's ability to recognize the end of a word as a clue to word meaning. Student's ability to recognize adjectives as words that describe.

Practice

Use BLM 17, Row 2–3.

Say: *Let's read the word* **life**. *Let's add* **–like**. *It reads:* **lifelike**. *It means "to seem alive." Remember, you can use the suffix* **–like** *to understand the meaning of a word, because the suffix* **–like** *means to "resembles." Write the suffix and root word to create the new word.*

Repeat the procedure with **book** to create **bookish**.

Apply

Use BLM 17, Row 4–5.

Say: *You read the word* **tickle**. *Add* **–ish** *at the end of the word and drop the silent* **-e**. *It reads:* **ticklish**. *What does it mean? It means "resembling being tickled." You can use the suffix* **–ish** *to understand the meaning of a word because the suffix* **–ish** *means to "resemble".*

Repeat the procedure with **child** to create **childlike**.

Conclusion

Ask: *What did we learn today? We learned that when we add the suffixes* **–like** *and* **–ish** *at the end of a word, they create new words that mean something else.*

Home Connection
Ask students to practice adding the suffixes **–like** and **–ish** to the ending of words to understand the meaning of the new words created. Have students identify words ending in **–like** and **–ish** with a family member and discuss their meaning.

✔ Formative Assessment

If the student completes each task correctly, proceed to the next skill in the sequence. If not, refer to suggested intervention 2.

Did the student…?	Intervention 2
Recognize and identify the beginning or end of a word?	• Point directly to the beginning and say, this is the beginning or the first part of the word ____. Point directly to the end of the word and say this is the end of the word____ or the last part of the word____. Say and point: Show me the beginning of the word. Show me the end of the word.
Understand the meaning **–like** is "to resemble."	• Say that to resemble something means to act or look like that item or person. Act out: childlike, childish, foolish, lifelike.
Read words?	• Point to each word and have students repeat, echo, then read it on their own while pointing to the word. Use the word in short sentences and explain its meaning to ensure student understanding.

Decode Words with Common Suffixes: -ways, -ward

Introduce

As students participate in this lesson, they will understand that affixes are a group of letters added at the beginning or end of a word to create a new word with a new meaning. Students will recognize that adjectives are words that are used to describe.

State Learning Goal

Say: *Today we will practice adding word parts to the end of words and recognize how it changes its meaning. We will learn we can use the word parts –**ways** and –**wards** as a clue to figure out the meaning of a word.*

Teach

Say: *A suffix is a group of letters that can be added to the end of a word.*

Ask: *To what part of a word is the suffix added? A suffix is added to the end of a word.*

Write the word **long** on the board. Write the suffix **–ways** on the board.

Say: *This is the word **long**. Read it with me: **long**. This is the suffix -**ways**. Read it with me -**ways**. I will add the suffix -**ways** at the end of the word do to make the word **longways**. The word **longways** means "in the manner of" when giving directions. For instance, we say, "You need to fold the paper longways." The suffix -**ways** changed the meaning of the word and created a new word **longways** that means "in the manner of" when giving directions.*

Write the word **west** on the board. Write the suffix **–ward** on the board.

Ask: *This is the word **west**. Read it with me: **west**. This is the suffix -**ward**. Read it with me: -**ward**. I will add the suffix -**ward** at the end of the word **west** to make the word **westward**. The word **westward** means "in the direction." For example, we say, "I will travel westward to get to my school." The suffix -**ward** changed the meaning of the word **west** to mean "in the direction of the west."*

Model

Use BLM 18, Row 1.

Say: *I read the word **side**. I add -**ways**. It reads: **sideways**. It means "in the manner of" when giving directions to go to the **side**. You can use the suffix -**ways** to understand the meaning of a word because the suffix -**ways** means "in the manner."*

Lesson Objectives

- Recognize and decode common affixes.
- Recognize that affixes that are placed at the beginning and end of a root/base word change the meaning of the word.
- Recognize that adverbs are words that tell more about verbs.

Metacognitive Strategy
- Selective Auditory Attention
- Use Deductive Thinking
- Generalize a Rule

Academic Language
- word ending, different meaning, prefix, base word, root word.
- Note: When using Latin-based suffixes the base word is called a root word.

Additional Materials
- Blackline Master 18

Pre-Assess

Student's ability to recognize a base or root word as the part of the word that contains meaning and can stand alone. Student's ability to recognize the end of a word as a clue to word meaning. Student's ability to recognize adverbs as words that tell more about verbs.

Practice

Use BLM 18, Row 2–3.

Say: *Let's read the word* **east.** *Let's add* **-ward.** *It reads:* **eastward.** *It means "to travel east." Remember, you can use the suffix* **-ward** *to understand the meaning of a word, because the suffix* **-ward** *means "in the direction of." Write the suffix and root word to create the new word.*

Repeat with **northward.**

Apply

Use BLM 18, Row 4–5.

Say: *You read the word* **home.** *Add* **-ward** *at the end of the word. It reads:* **homeward.** *What does it mean? It means "to go in the direction of home." You can use the suffix* **–ward** *to understand the meaning of a word because the suffix* **–ward** *means "in the direction."*

Repeat with the word **southward.**

Conclusion

Ask: *What did we learn today? We learned that when we add the suffixes* **-ways** *and* **–ward** *at the end of a word, they create new words that mean something else.*

Home Connection

Ask students to practice adding the suffixes **–ways** and **–ward** to the ending of words to understand the meaning of the new words created. Have students identify words ending in **–ways** and **–ward** with a family member and discuss their meaning.

✔ Formative Assessment

If the student completes each task correctly, proceed to the next skill in the sequence. If not, refer to suggested intervention 2.

Did the student…?	Intervention 2
Recognize and identify the beginning or end of a word?	• Point directly to the beginning and say, this is the beginning or the first part of the word ___. Point directly to the end of the word and say this is the end of the word___ or the last part of the word___. Say and point: Show me the beginning of the word. Show me the end of word.
Understand the meaning –ward is "in the direction."	• Say that the suffix *–ward* is often used to tell which direction someone or something is or should go.
Read words?	• Point to each word and have students repeat, echo, then read it on their own while pointing to the word. Use the word in short sentences and explain its meaning to ensure student understanding.

Decode Words with Common Prefixes: de-, dis-

Introduce

As students participate in this lesson, they will understand that prefixes are a group of letters added at the beginning of a word to create a new word with a new meaning. Students will recognize and generalize the understanding that the prefix **de-** and the prefix **dis-** mean *"not, opposite of."*

State Learning Goal

Say: *Today we will practice adding the prefix **de-** and the prefix **dis-**to the beginning of a verb or action word to recognize how it changes its meaning. We will learn we can use the prefix **de-** and the prefix **dis-** as a clue to figure out the meaning of a word.*

Teach

Say: *A prefix is a group of letters that can be added to the beginning of a word.*

Ask: *To what part of a word is the prefix added? A prefix is added to the beginning of a word.*

Write the word **forest** on the board. Write the prefix **de-** on the board.

Say: *This is the word **forest**. Read it with me: **forest**. This is the prefix **de-**. Read it with me: **de-**. I will add the prefix **de-** at the beginning of the word do to make the word **deforest**.*

Say: *Read it with me: **deforest**. **Deforest** means "not forested or cleared of trees." For instance, we say, "Cutting down all the trees will deforest the area." The prefix **de-** changed the meaning of the word. It can mean "to remove," "to reduce," or "the opposite of."*

Write the word **agree** on the board. Write the prefix **dis-** on the board.

Say: *This is the word **agree**. Read it with me: **agree**. This is the prefix **dis-**. Read it with me: **dis-**. I will add the prefix **dis-** at the beginning of the word **agree** to make the word **disagree**.*

Say: *Read it with me: **disagree**. **Disagree** means "the opposite of agree." For example, we say, "They disagree about what we should do." The prefix **dis-** changed the meaning of the word. It means "the opposite of." When you add the prefix to the beginning of a word, it creates a new word and changes its meaning.*

Ask: *What happens when you put a prefix at the beginning of a word? The meaning of the word changes.*

Lesson Objectives

- Recognize and decode common prefixes.
- Recognize that prefixes that are placed at the beginning of a root/base word change the meaning of the word.

Metacognitive Strategy
- Selective Auditory Attention
- Use Deductive Thinking
- Generalize a Rule

Academic Language
- word ending, different meaning, prefix, base word, root word

Additional Materials
- Blackline Master 19

Pre-Assess
Student's ability to recognize the beginning of a word as a clue to word meaning. Student's ability to recognize a base or root word as the part of the word that contains meaning and can stand alone.

Model

Use BLM 19, Row 1.

Say: *I read the word* **belief.** *I add* **dis-.** *It reads:* **disbelief.** *It means "not believe."* *You can use the prefix* **dis-** *to understand the meaning of a word, because the prefix* **dis-** *means "the opposite of." The write the root word and its prefix on the line.*

Practice

Use BLM 19, Row 2–4.

Say: *Let's read the word* **value.** *Let's add* **de-.** *It reads:* **devalue.** *It means "to remove value." Remember, you can use the prefix* **de-** *to understand the meaning of an action word or verb, because the prefix* **de-** *can mean "to remove."*

Repeat with the words **form** and **code.**

Apply

Blend Words

Use BLM 19, Row 5–7.

Say: *You read the word* **like.** *Add* **dis-** *at the beginning of the word. It reads:* **dislike.** *What does it mean? It means "the opposite of like." You can use the prefix* **dis-** *to understand the meaning of an action or verb because the prefix* **dis-** *means "the opposite of."*

Repeat with the words **honest** and **connect.**

Conclusion

Ask: *What did we learn today? We learned that when we add the prefix* **dis-** *and the prefix* **de-** *at the beginning of a word or verb, it creates a new word that means "not, opposite of" the original word.*

Home Connection

Ask students to practice adding the prefix **dis-** and the prefix **de-** to the beginning of action words or verbs to understand the meaning of the new word created. Have students identify action words or verbs to which the prefix **dis-** or the prefix **de-** can be added to create a new word with a family member.

✔ Formative Assessment

If the student completes each task correctly, proceed to the next skill in the sequence. If not, refer to suggested intervention 2.

Did the student…?	Intervention 2
Recognize and identify the beginning or end of a word?	• Point directly to the beginning and say, this is the beginning or the first part of the word **de-**. Point directly to the end of the word and say this is the end of the word place or the last part of the word defame. Say and point: Show me the beginning of the word. Show me the end of the word.
Understand the meaning of dis- and de-is "not, the opposite of?"	• Say that to disbelieve something means 'not to believe it." Then say that disagree means "not agreeing" Have students use these words in sentences to show they understand their meanings.
Read words?	• Point to each word and have students repeat, echo, then read it on their own while pointing to the word. Use the word in short sentences and explain its meaning to ensure student understanding.

Decode Words with Common Prefixes: mis-

Introduce

As students participate in this lesson, they will understand that prefixes are a group of letters added at the beginning of a word to create a new word with a new meaning. Students will recognize and generalize the understanding that the prefix **mis-** means "wrongly."

State Learning Goal

Say: *Today we will practice adding the prefix* **mis-** *to the beginning of a verb or action word to recognize how it changes its meaning. We will learn we can use the prefix* **mis-** *as a clue to figure out the meaning of a word.*

Teach

Say: *A prefix is a group of letters that can be added to the beginning of a word.*

Ask: *To what part of a word is the prefix added? A prefix is added to the beginning of a word.*

Write the word **behave** on the board. Write the prefix *mis-* on the board.

Say: *This is the word:* **behave.** *Read it with me:* **behave.** *This is the prefix:* **mis-.** *Read it with me:* **mis-.** *I will add the prefix* **mis-** *at the beginning of the word in order to make the word:* **misbehave.**

Say: *Read it with me:* **misbehave. Misbehave** *means "to behave in a way that is wrong." For instance, we say, "Don't misbehave in class. Listen to your teacher." The prefix* **mis-** *changed the meaning of the word and created a new word* **misbehave** *that means "to do something that is wrong."*

Write the word **count** on the board. Write the prefix **mis-** on the board.

Say: *This is the word:* **count.** *Read it with me:* **count.** *This is the prefix* **mis-.** *Read it with me:* **mis-.** *I will add the prefix* **mis-** *at the beginning of the word count to make the word* **miscount.**

Say: *Read it with me:* **miscount. Miscount** *means "to count wrongly." For example, we say, "You miscounted the plates. There should be four not five on the table." The prefix* **mis-** *changed the meaning of the word* **count** *and created a new word* **miscount,** *which means "to count wrongly."*

Ask: *What does* **misbehave** *mean? It means "to behave in a way that is wrong." What does* **miscount** *mean? It means "to count wrongly."*

Model

Use BLM 20, Row 1.

Say: *I read the word* **treat.** *I add* **mis-.** *It reads:* **mistreat.** *It means "to treat wrongly." You can use the prefix* **mis-** *to understand the meaning of an action word or verb, because the prefix* **mis-** *means to "do something wrongly" or to "do it incorrectly." Now write the root word and its prefix on the line.*

Lesson Objectives

- Recognize and decode common prefixes.
- Recognize that prefixes that are placed at the beginning of a root/base word change the meaning of the word.

Metacognitive Strategy
- Selective Auditory Attention
- Use Deductive Thinking
- Generalize a Rule

Academic Language
- word ending, different meaning, prefix, base word, root word

Additional Materials
- Blackline Master 20

Pre-Assess
Student's ability to recognize the beginning of a word as a clue to word meaning. Student's ability to recognize a base or root word as the part of the word that contains meaning and can stand alone.

Practice

Use BLM 20, Row 2–4.

Say: *Let's read the word* **dial**. *Let's add* **mis**–. *It reads:* **misdial**. *It means to "dial wrongly." Remember, you can use the prefix* **mis**– *to understand the meaning of an action word or verb, because the prefix* **mis**–*means "to do wrongly."*

Repeat with other words

Apply

Use BLM 20, Row 5–7.

Say: *You read the word* **lead**. *Add* **mis**- *at the beginning of the word. It reads:* **mislead**. *What does it mean? It means "lead wrongly." You can use the prefix* **mis**- *to understand the meaning of an action word or verb because the prefix* **mis**- *means "to do wrongly."*

Repeat with other words

Conclusion

Ask: *What did we learn today? We learned that when we add the prefix* **mis**– *at the beginning of a word or verb, it creates a new word that means doing something wrong.*

Home Connection

Ask students to practice adding the prefix **mis-** to he beginning of action words or verbs to understand the meaning of the new word created. Have students identify action words or verbs to which the prefix **mis-** can be added to create a new word with a family member.

✔ Formative Assessment

If the student completes each task correctly, proceed to the next skill in the sequence. If not, refer to suggested intervention 2.

Did the student…?	Intervention 2
Recognize and identify the beginning or end of a word?	• Point directly to the beginning and say, this is the beginning or the first part of the word **mis-**. Point directly to the end of the word and say this is the end of the word place or the last part of the word misplace. Say and point: Show me the beginning of the word. Show me end of the word.
Understand the meaning of mis- is "to do wrongly"	• Say that to mislabel something means 'to label it wrongly." Then dramatize an action. Draw something on the board and label it incorrectly. Say: Look, I mislabeled the picture. Then label it correctly.
Read words?	• Point to each word and have students repeat, echo, then read it on their own while pointing to the word. Use the word in short sentences and explain its meaning to ensure student understanding.

Decode Words with Common Prefixes: trans-, inter-

Introduce

As students participate in this lesson, they will understand that prefixes are a group of letters added at the beginning of a word to create a new word with a new meaning. Students will recognize and generalize the understanding that the prefix **trans-** means "across" and the prefix **inter-** means "between or among."

State Learning Goal

Say: *Today we will practice adding the prefix **trans-** to the beginning of a verb or action word to recognize how it changes its meaning. We will learn we can use the prefix **trans-** as a clue to figure out the meaning of a word. We will also practice adding the prefix **inter-** to the beginning of a verb or action word to recognize how it changes its meaning. We will also learn we can use the prefix **inter-** as a clue to figure out the meaning of a word.*

Teach

Say: *A prefix is a group of letters that can be added to the beginning of a word.*

Ask: *To what part of a word is the prefix added? A prefix is added to the beginning of a word.*

Write the word **Atlantic** on the board. Write the prefix **trans-** on the board.

Say: *This is the word **Atlantic**. Read it with me: **Atlantic**. This is the prefix **trans-**. Read it with me **trans-**. I will add the prefix **trans-** at the beginning of the word Atlantic to make the word **transatlantic**.*

Say: *Read it with me: **transatlantic**. **Transatlantic** means "to cross the Atlantic Ocean." For instance, we say, "I took a transatlantic trip." The prefix **trans-** changed the meaning of the word and created a new word **transatlantic** that means "to cross the Atlantic Ocean."*

Write the word **school** on the board. Write the prefix **inter-** on the board.

Ask: *This is the word **school**. Read it with me: **school**. This is the prefix **inter-**. Read it with me: **inter-**. I will add the prefix **inter-** at the beginning of the word school to make the word **interschool**.*

Say: *Read it with me: **interschool**. **Interschool** means "between or among schools." For example, we say, "We have an interschool party tomorrow after school. The prefix **inter-** changed the meaning of the word school and created a new word **interschool**, which means "between or among schools."*

Say: *By adding **inter-** to a noun, we create a new word, which means "between or among."*

Ask: *What does **transatlantic** mean? It means "to cross the Atlantic Ocean." What does **interschool** mean? It means "between or among schools."*

Lesson Objectives

- Recognize and decode common prefixes.
- Recognize that prefixes that are placed at the beginning of a root/base word change the meaning of the word.

Metacognitive Strategy
- Selective Auditory Attention
- Use Deductive Thinking
- Generalize a Rule

Academic Language
- word ending, different meaning, prefix, base word, root word

Additional Materials
- Blackline Master 21

Pre-Assess
Student's ability to recognize the beginning of a word as a clue to word meaning. Student's ability to recognize a base or root word as the part of the word that contains meaning and can stand alone.

Model

Use BLM 21, Row 1.

Say: *I read the word* **state.** *I add the prefix* **inter-**. *It reads:* **interstate.** *It means "between or among the states." You can use the prefix* **inter-** *to understand the meaning of a noun, because the prefix* **inter-** *means "between or among." Write the root word and its prefix on the line.*

Practice

Use BLM 21, Rows 2–4.

Say: *Let's read the word* **port.** *Let's add* **trans-**. *It reads:* **transport.** *It means to "carry across something". Remember, you can use the prefix* **trans-** *to understand the meaning of an noun, because the prefix* **trans-** *means "across." Write the root word and its prefix on the line.*

Repeat with other words.

Apply

Use BLM 21, Rows 5–7.

Say: *You read the word* **national.** *Add* **inter-** *at the beginning of the word. It reads:* **international.** *What does it mean? It means "between or among nations." You can use the prefix* **inter-** *to understand the meaning of a noun because the prefix* **inter-** *means "between or among." Then write the root word and its prefix on the line.*

Repeat with other words.

Conclusion

Ask: *What did we learn today? We learned that when we add the prefixes* **trans-** *and* **inter-** *at the beginning of nouns, they create new words that mean "across" or "between or among."*

Home Connection

Ask students to practice adding the prefixes **trans-** and **inter-** to the beginning of nouns to understand the meaning of the new words created. Have students identify nouns to which the prefix **trans-** and **inter-** can be added to create new words with a family member.

✔ Formative Assessment

If the student completes each task correctly, proceed to the next skill in the sequence. If not, refer to suggested intervention 2.

Did the student…?	Intervention 2
Recognize and identify the beginning or end of a word?	• Point directly to the beginning and say, this is the beginning or the first part of the word **inter-**. Point directly to the end of the word and say this is the end of the word place or the last part of the word interoffice. Say and point: Show me the beginning of the word. Show me end of the word.
Understand the meaning of trans- is "across"	• Say that transcontinental means "across continents." Have students repeat the word transcontinental with you and volunteers use a world map to show what the word means.
Read words?	• Point to each word and have students repeat, echo, then read it on their own while pointing to the word. Use the word in short sentences and explain its meaning to ensure student understanding.

Decode Words with Common Suffixes: -ment, -tion

Introduce

As students participate in this lesson, they will understand that suffixes are a group of letters added at the end of a word to create a new word with a new meaning. Students will recognize and generalize the understanding that the suffix **-ment** means "having the quality of" and the suffix **-tion** means "the act or process of."

State Learning Goal

Say: *Today we will practice adding the suffix* **-ment** *to the end of a of a verb to recognize how it changes its part of speech to a noun and also changes its meaning. We will learn we can use the suffix* **-ment** *as a clue to figure out the meaning of a word. We will also practice adding the suffix* **-tion** *to the end of a verb to recognize how it changes its part of speech to a noun and also changes its meaning. We will also learn we can use the suffix* **-tion** *as a clue to figure out the meaning of a word.*

Teach

Say: *A suffix is a group of letters that can be added to the end of a word.*

Ask: *To what part of a word is the suffix added? A suffix is added to the end of a word.*

Write the word **govern** on the board. Write the suffix **-ment** on the board.

Say: *This is the word* **government***. Read it with me:* **government***. This is the suffix* **-ment***. Read it with me* **-ment***. I will add the suffix* **-ment** *at the end of the word* **govern** *to make the word* **government***.*

Say: *Read it with me:* **government***.* **Government** *means "the act of ruling a country, state, etc." For instance, we say, "We have a democratic government." The suffix* **-ment** *changed the meaning of the verb govern and created a noun* **government** *that means "the act of ruling a country, state, etc."*

Write the word **direct** on the board. Write the suffix **-tion** on the board.

Say: *This is the word* **direct***. Read it with me:* **direct***. This is the suffix* **-tion***. Read it with me:* **-tion***. I will add the suffix* **-tion** *at the end of the word* **direct** *to make the word* **direction***.*

Say: *Read it with me:* **direction***.* **Direction** *means "the act of directing or guiding." For example, we say, "We were given lots of direction to do the project." The suffix* **-tion** *changed the meaning of the verb direct and created a noun* **direction** *that means "the act of directing or guiding."*

Say: *When you add the suffix to the ending of a word, it creates a new word and changes its meaning.*

Ask: *What does* **government** *mean? It means "the act of ruling a country, state, etc." What does* **direction** *mean? It means "the act of directing or guiding."*

Lesson Objectives

- Recognize and decode common suffixes.
- Recognize that suffixes that are placed at the end of a root/base word change the meaning of the word.

Metacognitive Strategy
- Selective Auditory Attention
- Use Deductive Thinking
- Generalize a rule

Academic Language
- word ending, different meaning, suffix, base word, root word

Additional Materials
- Blackline Master 22

Pre-Assess
Student's ability to recognize the end of a word as a clue to word meaning. Student's ability to recognize a base or root word as the part of the word that contains meaning and can stand alone.

Model

Use BLM 22, Row 1.

Say: *I read the word* **adopt**. *I add* **-ion**. *It reads:* **adoption**. *It means "having the quality of adopting or taking and using as one's own." You can use the suffix* **-ion** *to understand the meaning of a word, because the suffix* **-ion** *means "having the quality of." Now write the root word and its suffix on the line.*

Practice

Use BLM 22, Rows 2–4.

Say: *Let's read the word* **develop**. *Let's add* **-ment**. *It reads:* **development**. *It means to "the act or process of developing or bring something into being." Remember, you can use the suffix* **-ment** *to understand the meaning of a word, because the suffix* **-ment** *means "the act or process of." Now write the root word and its suffix on the line.*

Apply

Use BLM 22, Rows 5–7.

Say: *You read the word* **announce**. *Add* **-ment** *at the end of the word. It reads:* **announcement**. *What does it mean? It means "having the quality of announcing." You can use the suffix* **-ment** *to understand the meaning of a word because the suffix* **-ment** *means to "having the quality of." Now write the root word and its suffix on the line.*

Repeat with other words.

Conclusion

Ask: *What did we learn today? We learned that when we add the suffixes* **-ment** *and* **-tion** *at the end of verbs, they create new words, nouns, that mean "the act or process of" or "having the quality of."*

Home Connection

Ask students to practice adding the suffixes **-ment-** and **-tion** to the end of words to understand the meaning of the new words created. Have students identify verbs to which the suffixes **-ment** and **-tion** can be added to create new words that become nouns, with a family member.

✔ Formative Assessment

If the student completes each task correctly, proceed to the next skill in the sequence. If not, refer to suggested intervention 2.

Did the student…?	Intervention 2
Recognize and identify the beginning or end of a word?	• Point directly to the end of the word. Say this is the end of the word **-ment** or the last part of the word payment. Point to the beginning and say, this is the beginning or the first part of the word
Understand the meaning of -tion is "the act of"?	• Say that eruption means "the act or process of erupting." Have students repeat the word eruption with you and dramatize an eruption.
Read words?	• Point to each word and have students repeat, echo, then read it on their own while pointing to the word. Use the word in short sentences and explain its meaning to ensure student understanding.

Decode Words with Common Prefixes: anti-

Introduce

As students participate in this lesson, they will understand that prefixes are a group of letters added at the beginning of a word to create a new word with a new meaning. Students will recognize and generalize the understanding that the prefix **anti-** means "against."

State Learning Goal

Say: *Today we will practice adding the prefix to the beginning of a verb or action word to recognize how it changes its meaning. We will learn we can use the prefix* **anti-** *as a clue to figure out the meaning of a word.*

Teach

Say: *A prefix is a group of letters that can be added to the beginning of a word.*

Ask: *To what part of a word is the prefix added? A prefix is added to the beginning of a word.*

Write the word **hero** on the board. Write the prefix **anti-** on the board.

Say: *This is the word* **hero.** *Read it with me:* **hero.** *This is the prefix* **anti-.** *Read it with me* **anti-.** *I will add the prefix* **anti-** *at the beginning of the word* **hero** *to make the word* **antihero.** *The word* **antihero** *means "the opposite of a hero." For instance, we say, "The Joker is the antihero of Batman." The prefix* **anti-** *changed the meaning of the word* **hero** *and created a new word* **antihero** *that means "the opposite of a hero."*

Write the word **social** on the board. Write the prefix **anti-** on the board.

Say: *This is the word* **social.** *Read it with me:* **social.** *This is the prefix* **anti-.** *I will add the prefix* **anti-** *at the beginning of the word* **social** *to make the word* **antisocial.** *The word* **antisocial** *means "not social." For example, we say, "My uncle is antisocial because he doesn't like to be around other people." The prefix* **anti-** *changed the meaning of the word* **social** *and created a new word* **antisocial,** *which means "not social."*

Model

Use BLM 23, Row 1.

Say: *Read the word* **anxiety.** *Let's add* **anti-.** *It reads:* **antianxiety** *It means "not anxious." You can use the prefix* **anti-** *to understand the meaning of words, because the prefix* **anti-** *means "the opposite." Write the prefix to create the new word. Also write the new word.*

Lesson Objectives

- Recognize and decode common prefixes.
- Recognize that prefixes are placed at the beginning of a root/base word change the meaning of the word.

Metacognitive Strategy
- Selective Auditory Attention
- Use Deductive Thinking
- Generalize a Rule

Academic Language
- word ending, different meaning, prefix, base word, root word
- Note: When using Latin-based suffixes the base word is called a root word.

Additional Materials
- Blackline Master 23

Pre-Assess
Student's ability to recognize the beginning of a word as a clue to word meaning. Student's ability to recognize a base or root word as the part of the word that contains meaning and can stand alone.

Practice

Use BLM 23, Row 2–3.

Say: *Let's read the word* **freeze**. *Let's add* **anti-**. *It reads:* **antifreeze**. **Antifreeze** *is the name of a solution to keep cars from freezing and not running. Remember, you can use the prefix* **anti-** *to understand the meaning of a word because the prefix* **anti-** *means "the opposite." Write the prefix to create the new word. Also write the new word.*

Repeat for the word **antibody**.

Apply

Use BLM 20, Row 4–5.

Say: *You read the word* **theft**. *Add* **anti-** *at the beginning of the word. It reads:* **antitheft**. *What does it mean? It means "hard to steal." You can use the prefix* **anti-** *to understand the meaning of a word because the prefix* **anti-** *means the "opposite of." Write the prefix to create the new word. Also write the new word.*

Repeat for the word **antivenom**.

Conclusion

Ask: *What did we learn today? We learned that when we add the prefix* **anti-** *at the beginning of a word, it creates a new word that means* **not** *or the opposite of the word.*

Home Connection

Ask students to practice adding **anti-** to the beginning of words to understand the meaning of the new word created. Have students identify words to which the prefix **anti-** can be added to create a new word with a family member.

✔ Formative Assessment

If the student completes each task correctly, proceed to the next skill in the sequence. If not, refer to suggested intervention 2.

Did the student…?	Intervention 2
Recognize and identify the beginning or end of a word?	• Point directly to the beginning and say, this is the beginning or the first part of the word ____. Point directly to the end of the word and say this is the end of the word____ or the last part of the word____. Say and point: Show me the beginning of the word. Show me the end of the word.
Understand the meaning of the prefix that means the "opposite of?"	• Say that the opposite of something is different than the original. Then dramatize an action showing the opposite of a word.
Read words?	• Point to each word and have students repeat, echo, then read it on their own while pointing to the word. Use the word in short sentences and explain its meaning to ensure student understanding.

Decode Words with Common Prefixes: sub-

Introduce

As students participate in this lesson, they will understand that prefixes are a group of letters added at the beginning of a word to create a new word with a new meaning. Students recognize and generalize the understanding that the prefix **sub-** means "under."

State Learning Goal

Say: *Today we will practice adding the prefix* **sub-** *to the beginning of a verb or action word to recognize how it changes its meaning. We will learn we can use the prefix* **sub-** *as clues to figure out the meaning of a word.*

Teach

Say: *A prefix is a group of letters that can be added to the beginning of a word.*

Ask: *To what part of a word is the prefix added? A prefix is added to the beginning of a word.*

Write the word **marine** on the board. Write the prefix **sub-** on the board.

Say: *This is the word* **marine.** *Read it with me:* **marine.** *This is the prefix* **sub-** *Read it with me* **sub-**. *I will add the prefix* **sub-** *at the beginning of the word* **marine** *to make the word* **submarine.** *The word* **submarine** *means "a vessel used underwater." For instance, we say, "The submarine dove deep under the ocean's surface, to show that* **submarine** *means "a vessel used underwater."*

Write the word **freezing** on the board. Write the prefix **sub-** on the board.

Say: *This is the word* **freezing.** *Read it with me:* **freezing.** *This is the prefix* **sub-**. *I will add the prefix* **sub-** *at the beginning of the word* **freezing** *to make the word* **subfreezing.** *The word* **subfreezing** *means "below freezing."*

Model

Use BLM 24, Row 1.

Say: *I read the word* **merge.** *I add* **sub-** *so that it reads:* **submerge.** *It means "underwater." You can use the prefix* **sub-** *to understand the meaning of a word. Write the prefix to create the new word. Also write the new word.*

Lesson Objectives

- Recognize and decode common prefixes.
- Recognize that prefixes that are placed at the beginning of a root/base word change the meaning of the word.

Metacognitive Strategy
- Selective Auditory Attention
- Use Deductive Thinking
- Generalize a Rule

Academic Language
- word ending, different meaning, prefix, base word, root word
- Note: When using Latin-based suffixes the base word is called a root word.

Additional Materials
- Blackline Master 24

Pre-Assess
Student's ability to recognize the beginning of a word as a clue to word meaning. Student's ability to recognize a base or root word as the part of the word that contains meaning and can stand alone.

Practice

Use BLM 24, Row 2–3.

Say: *Let's read the word* **due**. *Let's add* **sub-**. *It reads:* **subdue**. *It means "to put under control." Remember, you can use the prefix* **sub-** *to understand the meaning of words. Write the prefix to create the new word. Also write the new word.*

Repeat with the word **submarine**.

Apply

Use BLM 24, Row 4–5.

Say: *You read the word* **way**. *Add* **sub-** *at the beginning of the word. It reads:* **subway**. *What does it mean? It means "a passageway under ground." You can use the prefix* **sub-** *to understand the meaning of words. Write the prefix to create the new word. Also write the new word.*

Repeat with the word **subtopic**.

Conclusion

Ask: *What did we learn today? We learned that when we add the prefix* **sub-** *at the beginning of a word, it changes the meaning of that word.*

Home Connection

Ask students to practice adding the prefixes **sub-** and **semi-** to the beginning of words to understand the meaning of the new word created. Have students identify words to which the prefixes **sub-** and **semi-** can be added to create a new word with a family member.

✔ Formative Assessment

If the student completes each task correctly, proceed to the next skill in the sequence. If not, refer to suggested intervention 2.

Did the student…?	Intervention 2
Recognize and identify the beginning or end of a word?	• Point directly to the beginning and say, this is the beginning or the first part of the word ___. Point directly to the end of the word and say this is the end of the word___ or the last part of the word___. Say and point: Show me the beginning of the word. Show me the end of the word.
Understand the meaning, **sub-** is "under"?	• Say that something that is under is the opposite of above. Then dramatize or show items under something else.
Read words?	• Point to each word and have students repeat, echo, then read it on their own while pointing to the word. Use the word in short sentences and explain its meaning to ensure student understanding.

Decode Words with Common Prefixes: in-, im-, ir-

Introduce

As students participate in this lesson, they will understand that prefixes are a group of letters added at the beginning of a word to create a new word with a new meaning. Students will recognize and generalize the understanding that the prefix **in-** means "not" or "opposite of." The same understanding is true for the prefixes **im-** and **ir-**.

State Learning Goal

Say: *Today we will practice adding the prefix to the beginning of a verb or action word to recognize how it changes its meaning. We will learn we can use the prefixes **in-**, **im-**, and **ir-** as clues to figure out the meaning of a word.*

Teach

Say: *A prefix is a group of letters that can be added to the beginning of a word.*

Ask: *To what part of a word is the prefix added? A prefix is added to the beginning of a word.*

Write the word **complete** on the board. Write the prefix **in-** on the board.

Say: *This is the word **complete**. Read it with me: **complete**. This is the prefix **in-**. Read it with me **in-**. I will add the prefix **in-** at the beginning of the word to make the word **incomplete**. The word **incomplete** means "not complete." For instance, we say, "My homework is incomplete." The prefix **in-** changed the meaning of the word and created a new word **incomplete,** which means "not complete."*

Write the word **polite** on the board. Write the prefix **im-** on the board.

Say: *I will add the prefix **im-** at the beginning of the word **polite** to make the word **impolite**. The word **impolite** means "not polite." For example, we say, "It is **impolite** to eat with your mouth open." The prefix **im-** changed the meaning of the word **polite** and created a new word **impolite**, which means "not **polite**."*

Repeat the procedure with **irregular**.

Model

Use BLM 25, Row 1.

Say: *I read the word **correct**. Let's add **in-**. It reads: **incorrect**. It means "not correct." You can use the prefix **in-** to understand the meaning of words, because the prefix **in-** means "not" or "opposite of." Add the prefix to the root word, and write out the new word this creates.*

Lesson Objectives

- Recognize and decode common prefixes.
- Recognize that prefixes that are placed at the beginning of a root/base word change the meaning of the word.

Metacognitive Strategy
- Selective Auditory Attention
- Use Deductive Thinking
- Generalize a rule

Academic Language
- word ending, different meaning, prefix, base word, root word
- Note: When using Latin-based suffixes the base word is called a root word.

Additional Materials
- Blackline Master 25

Pre-Assess
Student's ability to recognize the beginning of a word as a clue to word meaning. Student's ability to recognize a base or root word as the part of the word that contains meaning and can stand alone.

Practice

Use BLM 25, Row 2–3.

Say: *Let's read the word* **perfect.** *Let's add* **im-.** *It reads:* **imperfect.** *It means to "not perfect." Remember, you can use the prefix* **im-** *to understand the meaning of a word because the prefix* **im-** *means "not" or "opposite of." Write the prefix to create the new word. Also write the new word.*

Repeat the procedure with **inactive**.

Apply

Use BLM 25, Row 4–5.

Say: *You read the word* **regular.** *Add* **ir-** *at the beginning of the word. It reads:* **irregular.** *What does it mean? It means "not regular." You can use the prefix* **ir-** *to understand the meaning of a word because the prefix* **ir-** *means to "not" or "opposite of." Write the prefix to create the new word. Also write the new word.*

Repeat the procedure with **irrelevant**.

Conclusion

Ask: *What did we learn today? We learned that when we add the prefixes* **in-,** **im-,** *and* **ir-** *at the beginning of a word, it creates a new word that means not, or the opposite of, the word.*

Home Connection

Ask students to practice adding **in-, im-,** and **ir-** to the beginning of words to understand the meaning of the new word created. Have students identify words to which the prefixes **in-, im-,** or **ir-** can be added to create a new word with a family member.

✔ **Formative Assessment**

If the student completes each task correctly, proceed to the next skill in the sequence. If not, refer to suggested intervention 2.

Did the student…?	Intervention 2
Recognize and identify the beginning or end of a word?	• Point directly to the beginning and say, this is the beginning or the first part of the word ___. Point directly to the end of the word and say this is the end of the word___ or the last part of the word___. Say and point: Show me the beginning of the word. Show me the end of the word.
Understand the meaning of the prefixes that mean "not" or "opposite of?"	• Say that the opposite of something is different than the original. Then dramatize an action showing the opposite of a word, such as polite and impolite.
Read words?	• Point to each word and have students repeat, echo, then read it on their own while pointing to the word. Use the word in short sentences and explain its meaning to ensure student understanding.

Decode Words with Common Suffixes: -able, -ible, -al

Introduce

As students participate in this lesson, they understand that suffixes are a group of letters added at the end of a root word to create a new word with a new meaning. Students recognize and generalize the understanding that the suffixes **–able** and **-ible** mean "able to" or "can be." Students generalize and generalize the understanding that the suffixes **-able** and **-ible** mean "able to" or "can be." Students will also recognize and generalize the understanding that the suffixes **–al** and **–ial** mean "having characteristic of."

State Learning Goal

Say: *Today we will practice adding the suffix **–able** and the suffix **-ible** to the end of a word to recognize how they change its meaning. We can use the suffix **–able** and the suffix **-ible** as clues to figure out the meaning of a word. Repeat for **–al** and **–ial**.*

Teach

Say: *A suffix is a group of letters that can be added to the end of a word.*

Ask: *To what part of a word is the suffix added? A suffix is added to the end of a word.*

Write the word **capable** on the board. Underline **–able**.

Say: *This is the word **capable**. Read it with me: **capable**. This is the suffix **–able**. Read it with me **-able**. The suffix **–able** is a word part in the word **capable**.*

Say: *Read it with me: **capable**. **Capable** means "one who is able to."*

Write the word **responsible** on the board. Underline **–ible**.

Say: *This is the word **responsible**. Read it with me: **responsible**. This is the suffix **–ible**. Read it with me:**-ible**. The suffix **–ible** is a word part in the word **responsible**.*

Say: *Read it with me: **responsible**. **Responsible** means "one who is able to make decisions."*

Say: *When you add a suffix to the end of a word, it changes the meaning of the word.*

Ask: *What happens when you add a suffix to the end of a word? The meaning of the word changes.*

Ask: *What does **capable** mean? It means "one who is able." What does **responsible** mean? It means "one who is able to make decisions."*

Lesson Objectives
- Recognize and decode common suffixes.
- Recognize that suffixes placed at the end of a root/base word change the meaning of the word.

Metacognitive Strategy
- Selective Auditory Attention
- Use Deductive Thinking
- Generalize a rule

Academic Language
- word ending, different meaning, suffix, base word, root word
- Note: When using Latin-based suffixes, the base word is called a root word.

Additional Materials
- Blackline Master 26

Pre-Assess
Student's ability to recognize the end of a word as a clue to word meaning Student's ability to recognize a base or root word as the part of the word that contains meaning and can stand alone.

Model

Use BLM 26, Row 1.

Say: *I read the word* **sensible.** *It has the word part* **–ible** *included at the end. It means "able to show good sense." I read the word* **detach.** *I add* **–able.** *It reads:* **detachable.** *It means "able to detach." You can use the suffix* **–ible** *and suffix* **–able** *to understand the meaning of a word.*

Repeat with other words.

Practice

Use BLM 26, Row 2–3.

Say: *Let's read the word* **respect.** *We add* **-able** *It reads:* **respectable.** *It means "able to be respected." Let's read the words* **horrible** *and* **terrible.** *Let's circle the suffixes.*

Repeat with the words **visible** and **incredible.**

Apply

Use BLM 26, Row 4–5.

Say: *You read the word* **accept.** *We add* **-able** *It reads:* **acceptable.** *It means "able to accept." Let's read the word* **suggest.** *We add* **-able.** *It means "able to be given a suggestion." You can use suffixes to understand the meaning of a word.*

Repeat with other words.

Conclusion

Say: *What did we learn today? We learned that when we add the suffix* **–able** *or the suffix* **–ible** *to the end of a word, it changes the meaning of the word. The suffixes* **–able** *and* **–ible** *both mean "able to."*

Home Connection

Ask students to practice adding **–able** and **–ible** to the end of words and to understand the meaning of the new word. Ask students to identify other words that have the suffix **-able** or **–ible** with a family member.

✔ Formative Assessment

If the student completes each task correctly, proceed to the next skill in the sequence. If not, refer to suggested intervention 2

Did the student…?	Intervention 2
Recognize and identify the end of a word?	• Point directly to the end of the word. Say this is the end of the word____ or the last part of the word____. Point to the beginning and say, this is the beginning or the first part of the word
Understand the meaning of **–able** and **–ible?**	• Show **–able** and **–ible** as similar categories. Have students sort words under **–able** and **–ible** as the meanings of each word is discussed.
Repeat words and phrases when asked?	• Point to the word and have students echo-read, then read it on their own while pointing to the word

Decode Words with Common Suffixes: -ant, -ent

Introduce

As students participate in this lesson, they will understand that suffixes are a group of letters added at the end of a root word to create a new word with a new meaning. Students will recognize and generalize the understanding that the suffixes **–ant** and **-ent** mean "one who." Students will generalize and generalize the understanding that the suffixes **-ant** and **-ent** mean "one who."

State Learning Goal

Say: *Today we will practice adding the suffix –ant and the suffix -ent to the end of a word to recognize how they change its meaning. We can use the suffix –ant and the suffix -ent as clues to figure out the meaning of a word.*

Teach

Say: *A suffix is a group of letters that can be added to the end of a word.*

Ask: *To what part of a word is the suffix added? A suffix is added to the end of a word.*

Write the word **defend** on the board. Write the suffix **-ant** on the board.

Say: *This is the word **defend**. Read it with me: **defend**. This is the suffix **–ant**. Read it with me **-ant**. I will add the suffix **-ant** at the end of the word defend to make the word **defendant**. The word **defendant** means "one who defends." The meaning of the word **defend** changed.*

Write the word **correspond** on the board. Write the suffix **–ent** on the board.

Say: *This is the word **correspond**. Read it with me: **correspond**. This is the suffix **–ent**. Read it with me: **-ent**. I will add the suffix **–ent** at the end of the word **correspond** to make the word **correspondent**. The word **correspond** means "one who corresponds." The meaning of the word **correspondent** has changed.*

Model

Use BLM 27, Row 1.

Say: *I read the word **depend**. I add **-ent** It reads: **dependent**. It means "relying on someone/something."*

Lesson Objectives

- Recognize and decode common suffixes.
- Recognize that suffixes placed at the end of a root/base word change the meaning of the word.

Metacognitive Strategy
- Selective Auditory Attention
- Use Deductive Thinking
- Generalize a Rule

Academic Language
- word ending, different meaning, prefix, base word, root word
- Note: When using Latin-based suffixes the base word is called a root word.

Additional Materials
- Blackline Master 27

Pre-Assess

Student's ability to recognize the end of a word as a clue to word meaning Student's ability to recognize a base or root word as the part of the word that contains meaning and can stand alone.

Practice

Use BLM 27, Row 2–3.

Say: *Let's read the word* **assist.** *We add* **-ant** *It reads:* **assistant.** *It means "one who assists." Let's read the word* **absorb.** *We add* **–ent.** *It reads:* **absorbent.** *It means "one that absorbs." You can use the suffix* **–ent** *and suffix* **–ant** *to understand the meaning of a word.*

Repeat with other words.

Apply

Use BLM 27, Row 4–5.

Say: *You read the word* **contest.** *We add* **-ant.** *It reads:* **contestant.** *It means "one who is in a contest." Let's read the word* **differ.** *We add* **-ent.** *It reads:* **different.** *It means "one that differs." You can use the suffixes* **-ent** *and* **-ant** *to understand the meaning of a word.*

Repeat with other words

Conclusion

Ask: *What did we learn today? We learned that when we add the suffix* **–ent** *or the suffix* **–ant** *to the end of a word, it changes the meaning of the word. The suffixes* **–ent** *and* **–ant** *both mean "one who."*

Home Connection

Ask students to practice adding **–ent** and **–ant** to the end of words and to understand the meaning of the new word. Ask students to identify other words that have the suffix **-ant** or **–ent** with a family member.

✔ Formative Assessment

If the student completes each task correctly, proceed to the next skill in the sequence. If not, refer to suggested intervention 2.

Did the student…?	Intervention 2
Recognize and identify the end of a word?	• Point directly to the end of the word. Say this is the end of the word____ or the last part of the word____. Point to the beginning and say, this is the beginning or the first part of the word
Understand the meaning of **-ant** and **-ent**?	Show **-ent** and **-ant** as similar categories. Have students sort words under **-ent** and **-ant** as the meanings of each word is discussed.
Repeat words and phrases when asked?	• Point to the word and have students echo-read, then read it on their own while pointing to the word

Decode Words with Common Suffixes: -ous , -eous, and -ious

Introduce

As students participate in this lesson, they will understand that suffixes are a group of letters added at the end of a word to create a new word with a new meaning. Students will recognize and generalize the understanding that the suffixes **-ous**, **-eous**, and **-ious** mean "having the quality of."

State Learning Goal

Say: *Today we will practice adding the suffixes **-ous**, **-eous**, and **-ious** to the end of a word to recognize how it changes its part of speech to an adjective and also changes its meaning. We will learn we can use the suffixes **-ous** , **-eous**, and -ious as clues to figure out the meanings of words.*

Teach

Say: *A suffix is a group of letters that can be added to the end of a word.*

Ask: *To what part of a word is the suffix added? A suffix is added to the end of a word.*

Write the word **danger** on the board. Write the suffix -**ous** on the board.

Say: *This is the word **danger**. Read it with me: **dangerous**. This is the suffix **-ous**. Read it with me **-ous**. I will add the suffix **-ous** at the end of the word **danger** to make the word **dangerous**. For instance, we say, "Riding a bike without a helmet is a dangerous thing to do." The suffix **-ous** changed the meaning of the noun **danger** and created an adjective **dangerous** that means "having the quality of danger."*

Write the word **fury** on the board. Write the suffix -**ious** on the board.

Say: *This is the word **fury**. Read it with me: **fury**. This is the suffix **-ious**. Read it with me: **-ious**. I will add the suffix **-ious** at the end of the word **fury** to make the word **furious**.*

Say: *Read it with me: **furious**. **Furious** means "having the quality of fury or anger." The suffix **-ious** changed the meaning of the noun **fury** and created an adjective **furious** which means "having the quality of fury or anger."*

Model

Use BLM 28, Row 1.

Say: *I read the word **joy**. I add **-ous**. It reads: **joyous**. It means "having the quality of joy or happiness." You can use the suffix **-ous** to understand the meaning of a word, because the suffix **–ous** means "having the quality of." Now write the root word and its suffix on the line.*

Lesson Objectives

- Recognize and decode common suffixes.
- Recognize that suffixes that are placed at the end of a root/base word change the meaning of the word.

Metacognitive Strategy
- Selective Auditory Attention
- Use Deductive Thinking
- Generalize a Rule

Academic Language
- word ending, different meaning, suffix, base word, root word

Additional Materials
- Blackline Master 28

Pre-Assess
Student's ability to recognize the end of a word as a clue to word meaning. Student's ability to recognize a base or root word as the part of the word that contains meaning and can stand alone.

Practice

Use BLM 28, Rows 2–4.

Say: *Let's read the word* **mystery.** *Let's add* **-ious.** *It reads:* **mysterious.** *It means "having the quality of mystery." Remember, you can use the suffix* **-ious** *to understand the meaning of a word, because the suffix* **–ious** *means "having the quality of." Now write the root word and its suffix on the line.*

Repeat with **ceremony** and **glory**.

Apply

Use BLM 28, Rows 5–7.

Say: *You read the word* **advantage.** *Add* **–ous** *at the end of the word. It reads:* **advantageous***. What does it mean? It means "having the quality of an advantage." You can use the suffix* **-ous** *to understand the meaning of a word because the suffix* **-ous** *means to "having the quality of." Now write the root word and its suffix on the line.*

Repeat with **gas** and **courtesy**.

Conclusion

Ask: *What did we learn today? We learned that when we add the suffixes* **-ous** *and* **-ious** *and* **–eous** *at the end of nouns, they create new words, adjectives, that mean "having the quality of."*

Home Connection
Ask students to practice adding the suffixes **–ous, -ious,** and **-eous** to the end of words to understand the meaning of the new words created. Have students identify nouns to which the suffixes **–ous, -ious,** and **-eous** can be added to create new words that become adjectives, with a family member.

✔ **Formative Assessment**

If the student completes each task correctly, proceed to the next skill in the sequence. If not, refer to suggested intervention 2.

Did the student…?	Intervention 2
Recognize and identify the beginning or end of a word?	• Point directly to the end of the word. Say this is the end of the word **-ous** or the last part of the word poisonous. Point to the beginning and say, this is the beginning or the first part of the word
Understand the meaning **–ous,** **--ious,** and **-eous** mean "having the quality of?"	• Say that luxurious means "have the quality of luxury or comfort." Have students repeat the word luxurious with you and name some things they think are luxurious.
Read words?	• Point to each word and have students repeat, echo, then read it on their own while pointing to the word. Use the word in short sentences and explain its meaning to ensure student understanding.

Decode Words with Common Suffixes: -ive , -ative, and -itive

Introduce

As students participate in this lesson, they will understand that suffixes are a group of letters added at the end of a word to create a new word with a new meaning. Students will recognize and generalize the understanding that the suffixes **-ive** , **-ative**, and **-itive** mean "having the quality of."

State Learning Goal

Say: *Today we will practice adding the suffixes* **-ive** *, * **-ative***, and* **-itive** *to the end of a word to recognize how it changes its part of speech to an adjective and also changes its meaning. We will learn we can use the suffixes* **-ive** *, * **-ative***, and –**itive** *as a clue to figure out the meanings of words.*

Teach

Say: *A suffix is a group of letters that can be added to the end of a word.*

Ask: *To what part of a word is the suffix added? A suffix is added to the end of a word.*

Write the word **adopt** on the board. Write the suffix -**ive** on the board.

Say: *This is the word* **adopt***. Read it with me:* **adopt***. This is the suffix* **-ive***. Read it with me* **-ive***. I will add the suffix* **-ive** *at the end of the word* **adopt** *to make the word* **adoptive***.*

Say: *Read it with me:* **adoptive***.* **Adoptive** *means "having the quality of being adopted." For instance, we say, "Tim loves his adoptive parents." The suffix* **-ive** *changed the meaning of the verb* **adopt** *and created an adjective* **adoptive** *that means "having the quality of being adopted."*

Write the word **talk** on the board. Write the suffix **-ative** on the board.

Say: *This is the word* **talk***. Read it with me:* **talk***. This is the suffix* **-ative***. Read it with me:* **-ative***. I will add the suffix* **-ative** *at the end of the word* **talk** *to make the word* **talkative***.*

Say: *Read it with me:* **talkative***.* **Talkative** *means "having the quality of talking a lot." For example, we say, "The talkative student raised his hand a lot in class." The suffix* **-ative** *changed the meaning of the verb talk and created an adjective* **talkative** *which means "having the quality of talking a lot."*

Repeat the procedure with the word **sense** and the suffix –**itive** on the board.

Lesson Objectives

- Recognize and decode common suffixes.
- Recognize that suffixes that are placed at the end of a root/base word change the meaning of the word.

Metacognitive Strategy
- Selective Auditory Attention
- Use Deductive Thinking
- Generalize a Rule

Academic Language
- word ending, different meaning, suffix, base word, root word

Additional Materials
- Blackline Master 28

Pre-Assess
Student's ability to recognize the end of a word as a clue to word meaning. Student's ability to recognize a base or root word as the part of the word that contains meaning and can stand alone.

Model

Use BLM 29, Row 1.

Say: *I read the word **protect**. I add **-ive**. It reads: **protective**. It means "having the quality of wanting to protect someone or something." You can use the suffix **-ive** to understand the meaning of a word, because the suffix **–ive** means "having the quality of." Now write the root word and its suffix on the line.*

Practice

Use BLM 29, Rows 2–4.

Say: *Let's read the word **add**. Let's add **-itive**. It reads: **additive**. It means "having the quality of being added." Remember, you can use the suffix **–itive** to understand the meaning of a word, because the suffix **–itive** means "having the quality of being added." Now write the root word and its suffix on the line.*

Repeat with **define** and **compete**.

Apply

Use BLM 29, Rows 5–7.

Say: *You read the word **imagine**. Add **–ative** at the end of the word. It reads: **imaginative**. What does it mean? It means "having the quality of imagination." You can use the suffix **-ative** to understand the meaning of a word because the suffix **-ative** means to "having the quality of." Now write the root word and its suffix on the line.*

Repeat with **compare** and **cure**.

Conclusion

Ask: *What did we learn today? We learned that when we add the suffixes **–ive**, **-ative**, and **-itive** at the end of nouns, they create new words, adjectives, that mean "having the quality of."*

Home Connection

Ask students to practice adding the suffixes **–ive, -ative,** and **-itive** to the end of words to understand the meaning of the new words created. Have students work with a family member to identify nouns to which the suffixes **–ive, -ative,** and **-itive** can be added.

✔ Formative Assessment

If the student completes each task correctly, proceed to the next skill in the sequence. If not, refer to suggested intervention 2.

Did the student...?	Intervention 2
Recognize and identify the beginning or end of a word?	• Point directly to the end of the word. Say this is the end of the word • **-ive, ative, itive** or the last part of the word creative, imaginative, and competitive. Point to the beginning and say, "This is the beginning or the first part of the word."
Understand the meaning **–ives, –ative,** and **–itive** mean "having the quality of"	• Say that **–ives, –ative,** and **–itive** all mean "have the quality of." Have students name a word with each suffix and say what the words mean.
Read words?	• Point to each word and have students repeat, echo, then read it on their own while pointing to the word. Use the word in short sentences and explain its meaning to ensure student understanding.

Decode Words with Common Suffixes: -ology, -graphic, and -graphy

Introduce

As students participate in this lesson, they will understand that suffixes are a group of letters added at the end of a root word to create a new word with a new meaning. Students will recognize and generalize the understanding that the suffix **–ology** means "the study of." Students will recognize and generalize the understanding that the suffixes -**graphic** and -**graphy** mean "writing" or "letter."

State Learning Goal

Say: *Today we will practice adding the suffix **–ology**, -**graphic**, and -**graphy** to the end of a word to recognize how they change its meaning. We can use the suffix **–ology**, -**graphic**, and the suffix **–graphy** as clues to figure out the meaning of a word.*

Teach

Say: *A suffix is a group of letters that can be added to the end of a word.*

Ask: *To what part of a word is the suffix added? A suffix is added to the end of a word.*

Write the word **music** on the board. Write the suffix **–ology**.

Say: *This is the word **music**. Read it with me: **music**. This is the suffix **–ology**. Read it with me -**ology**. The suffix **–ology** means "the study of."*

Say: *Read it with me: **musicology**. **Musicology** means "the study of music."*

Write the word **bio** on the board. Underline **–graphy**.

Say: *This is the root word **bio**. Read it with me: **bio**. This is the suffix **–graphy**. Read it with me: -**graphy**. The suffix **–graphy** is a word part in the word **biography**. The word **biography** means "a piece of writing about someone's life."*

Ask: *What happens when you add a suffix to the end of a word? The meaning of the word changes.*

Ask: *What does **musicology** mean? It means "the study of music." What does **biography** mean? It means "a piece of writing about someone's life."*

Model

Use BLM 30, Row 1.

Say: *I read the word **geology**. It has the word part **–ology** included at the end. It means "the study of the environment." You can use the suffix **–ology** to understand the meaning of a word.*

Lesson Objectives

- Recognize and decode common suffixes.
- Recognize that suffixes placed at the end of a root/base word change the meaning of the word.

Metacognitive Strategy
- Selective Auditory Attention
- Use Deductive Thinking
- Generalize a Rule

Academic Language
- word ending, different meaning, suffix, base word, root word.
- Note: When using Latin-based suffixes, the base word is called a root word.

Additional Materials
- Blackline Master 30

Pre-Assess
Student's ability to recognize the end of a word as a clue to word meaning Student's ability to recognize a base or root word as the part of the word that contains meaning and can stand alone.

Practice

Use BLM 30, Row 2–4.

Say: *Let's look at the root word* **bio.** *We can add the suffix* **–ology,** *which means "the study of," to the end of this root. Now, let's read the entire word:* **biology.** *We can use our understanding of the suffix* **–ology** *to understand the meaning of a word* **biology** *as "the study of life."*

Repeat the procedure with **photo (photographic)** and **video (videography).**

Apply

Use BLM 30, Row 5–7.

Say: *You can look at the root word* **zoo.** *We can add the suffix* **–ology,** *which means "the study of," to the end of this root. Now, let's read the entire word:* **zoology.** *We can use our understanding of suffix* **–ology** *to understand the meaning of a word* **zoology** *as "the study of animals."*

Repeat the procedure with **ocean (oceanography)** and **criminal (criminology).**

Conclusion

Ask: *What did we learn today? We learned that when we add the suffix* **-ology, -graphic,** *or* **-graphy** *to the end of a word, it changes the meaning of the word. The suffix* **-ology** *means "study of" and the suffixes* **-graphic** *and* **-graphy** *mean "writing or letters."*

Home Connection

Ask students to practice adding **–ology, -graphic,** and **–graphy** to the end of words and to understand the meaning of the new word. Ask students to identify other words that have the suffix **–ology, -graphic,** or **–graphy** with a family member.

✔ **Formative Assessment**

If the student completes each task correctly, proceed to the next skill in the sequence. If not, refer to suggested intervention 2.

Did the student…?	Intervention 2
Recognize and identify the end of a word?	• Point directly to the end of the word. Say this is the end of the word____ or the last part of the word____. Point to the beginning and say, this is the beginning or the first part of the word
Understand the meaning of **-ology, -graphic,** and **-graphy**?	• Create a three-column chart and have students sort **-ology, -graphic,** and **-graphy** words into the three columns.
Repeat words and phrases when asked?	• Point to the word and have students echo-read, then read it on their own while pointing to the word.

Decode Words with Common Suffixes: -phobia, -scope

Introduce

As students participate in this lesson, they will understand that suffixes are a group of letters added at the end of a root word to create a new word with a new meaning. Students will recognize and generalize the understanding that the suffix **–phobia** means "fear of." Students will recognize and generalize the understanding that the suffix **-scope** means "view" or "examine."

State Learning Goal

Say: *Today we will practice adding the suffixes* **–phobia** *and* **–scope** *to the ends of words to recognize how they change their meanings. We can use the suffix* **–scope** *and the suffix* **–phobia** *as clues to figure out the meanings of words.*

Teach

Say: *A suffix is a group of letters that can be added to the end of a word.*

Ask: *To what part of a word is the suffix added? A suffix is added to the end of a word.*

Write the word **thermophobia** on the board. Underline the suffix **–phobia**.

Say: *This is the word* **thermophobia**. *Read it with me:* **thermophobia**. *It has the word part* **–phobia**. *Read it with me* **-phobia**. *The suffix* **–phobia** *means "the fear of."*

Say: *Read it with me:* **thermophobia**. **Thermo-** *means "heat," so* **thermophobia** *means "the fear of heat."*

Write the word **microscope** on the board. Underline **–scope**.

Say: *This is the word* **microscope**. *Read it with me:* **microscope**. *This is the suffix* **–scope**. *Read it with me:* **-scope**. *The suffix* **–scope** *is a word part in the word* **microscope**.

Say: *Read it with me:* **microscope**. *I know that* **micro-** *means "small," so* **microscope** *must mean "a device to view something small."*

Ask: *What does* **thermophobia** *mean? It means "the fear of heat." What does* **microscope** *mean? It means "a device to view something small."*

Model

Use BLM 31, Row 1.

Say: *Let's read the word part **tele-***. *We can add the suffix **–scope** to the end. I know that **tele-** means "from a distance." So when I put the two word parts together, they form the word **telescope***. *This word describes a device that lets you see things from a great distance. You can use the suffix **–scope** to understand the meaning of a word.*

Practice

Use BLM 31, Row 2–4.

Say: *Let's read the word part **aqua-***. *We can add the suffix **–phobia** to the end. When I put the two word parts together, they form the word **aquaphobia***. *I know that **aqua-** means "water." I know the suffix **–phobia** means "fear of." So **aquaphobia** must mean "fear of water." We can use the suffix **–phobia** and suffix **–scope** to understand the meaning of a word.*

Repeat the procedure with **claustro– (claustrophobia)** and **arachno– (arachnophobia)**.

Apply
Blend Words

Use BLM 31, Row 5–7.

Say: *Let's read the word **night***. *Let's add the suffix **–scope** to the end. It makes **nightscope***. *It describes a device that lets you see things at night. You can use suffixes to understand the meaning of a word.*

Repeat the procedure with **stetho (stethoscope)** and **peri (periscope)**.

Conclusion

Ask: *What did we learn today? We learned that when we add the suffix **–phobia** or **–scope** to the end of a word, it changes the meaning of the word. The suffix -phobia means "fear of" and the suffix **–scope** means "view" or "examine."*

Home Connection

Ask students to practice adding **–phobia** and **–scope** to the end of words and to understand the meaning of the new word. Ask students to identify other words that have the suffix **–phobia,** or **–scope** with a family member.

✔ **Formative Assessment**

If the student completes each task correctly, proceed to the next skill in the sequence. If not, refer to suggested intervention 2.

Did the student…?	Intervention 2
Recognize and identify the end of a word?	• Point directly to the end of the word. Say this is the end of the word____ or the last part of the word____. Point to the beginning and say, this is the beginning or the first part of the word.
Understand the meaning of –phobia and –scope?	• Create a two-column chart and have students sort –phobia and –scope words into the three columns.
Repeat words and phrases when asked?	• Point to the word and have students echo-read, then read it on their own while pointing to the word.

Decode Words with Common Suffixes: -ory, -ist

Lesson Objectives

- Recognize and decode common suffixes.
- Recognize that suffixes placed at the end of a root/base word change the meaning of the word.

Metacognitive Strategy
- Selective Auditory Attention
- Use Deductive Thinking
- Generalize a Rule

Academic Language
- word ending, different meaning, suffix, base word, root word.
- Note: When using Latin-based suffixes, the base word is called a root word.

Additional Materials
- Blackline Master 32

Pre-Assess
Student's ability to recognize the end of a word as a clue to word meaning. Student's ability to recognize a base or root word as the part of the word that contains meaning and can stand alone.

Introduce

As students participate in this lesson, they will understand that suffixes are a group of letters added at the end of a root word to create a new word with a new meaning. Students will recognize and generalize the understanding that the suffix **–ory** means "place for" and **–ist** means "one who practices."

State Learning Goal

Say: T*oday we will practice adding the suffix* **–ory** *and* **-ist** *to the end of a word to recognize how they change its meaning. We can use the suffix* **–ory** *and the suffix* **–ist** *as clues to figure out the meaning of a word.*

Teach

Say: *A suffix is a group of letters that can be added to the end of a word.*

Ask: *To what part of a word is the suffix added? A suffix is added to the end of a word.*

Write the word **migratory** on the board. Underline the suffix **–ory**.

Say: *This is the word* **migratory**. *Read it with me:* **migratory**. *It has the word part* **–ory**. *Read it with me* **–ory**. *The suffix* **–ory** *means "relating to." I know that to* **migrate** *means to move from place to place. So,* **migratory** *must mean "related to moving to place to place."*

Write the word **art** on the board. Write the suffix **–ist** on the board.

Say: *This is the word* **art**. *Read it with me:* **art**. *This is the suffix* **–ist**. *Read it with me:* **-ist**. *When I put the two together, they form the word* **artist**.

Say: *Read it with me:* **artist**. *It means "a person who practices art."*

Model

Use BLM 32, Row 1–2.

Say: *I read the word* **sense**. *I drop the* **–e** *and add* **–ory**. *It reads:* **sensory**. *It means "related to the senses." I read the word* **cycle**. *I add* **–ist**. *It reads:* **cyclist**. *It means "one who cycles." You can use the suffix* **–ory** *and suffix* **–ist** *to understand the meaning of a word.*

Practice

Use BLM 32, Row 3–4.

Say: *Let's read the word* **supervisory**. *We underline the word part* **–ory**. *It reads:* **supervisory**. *It means "related to supervising." Let's read the word* **chemist**. *We underline* **–ist**. *It reads:* **chemist**. *It means "one who studies chemistry." You can use the suffix* **–ory** *and suffix* **–ist** *to understand the meaning of a word.*

Apply
Blend Words
Use BLM 32, Row 5–6.

Say: *You can read the word* **advise**. *You can drop the* **–e** *and add* **–ory**. *Now you can read:* **advisory**. *It means "related to advising." Now, read the word* **essay**. *You can add* **–ist**. *It reads:* **essayist**. *It means "a person who practices essays." You can use the suffix* **–ory** *and suffix* **–ist** *to understand the meaning of a word.*

Conclusion
Ask: *What did we learn today? We learned that when we add the suffix* **–ory** *or* **–ist** *to the end of a word, it changes the meaning of the word. The suffix* **–ory** *means "related to" and the suffix* **–ist** *means "one who practices."*

Home Connection
Ask students to practice adding **–ory** and **–ist** to the end of words and to understand the meaning of the new word. Ask students to identify other words that have the suffix **–ory** or **–ist** with a family member.

✔ Formative Assessment

If the student completes each task correctly, proceed to the next skill in the sequence. If not, refer to suggested intervention 2.

Did the student…?	Intervention 2
Recognize and identify the end of a word?	• Point directly to the end of the word. Say this is the end of the word____ or the last part of the word____. Point to the beginning and say, this is the beginning or the first part of the word.
Understand the meaning of **–ory** and **–ist**?	• Create a two-column chart and have students sort **–ory** and **–ist** words into the three columns.
Repeat words and phrases when asked?	• Point to the word and have students echo-read, then read it on their own while pointing to the word

Decode Words with Common Suffixes: -ate, -fy

Introduce

As students participate in this lesson, they will understand that suffixes are a group of letters added at the end of a root word to create a new word with a new meaning. Students will recognize and generalize the understanding that the suffix **–ate** means "to make" and **–fy** means "to make into."

State Learning Goal

Say: *Today we will practice adding the suffix* **–ate** *and* **–fy** *to the end of a word to recognize how they change its meaning. We can use the suffix* **–ate** *and the suffix* **–fy** *as clues to figure out the meaning of a word.*

Teach

Say: *A suffix is a group of letters that can be added to the end of a word.*

Ask: *To what part of a word is the suffix added? A suffix is added to the end of a word.*

Write the word **animate** on the board. Underline the suffix **–ate**.

Say: *This is the word* **animate.** *Read it with me:* **animate.** *It has the word part* **–ate**. *Read it with me* **–ate**. *The suffix* **–ate** *means "to make."*

Say: *Read it with me:* **animate.** *It means "to make something alive."*

Write the word **clarify** on the board. Underline the suffix **–fy**.

Say: *This is the word* **clarify**. *Read it with me:* **clarify**. *This is the suffix* **–fy.** *Read it with me:* **–fy**. *When I put the two together, it forms* **clarify**. *It means "to make clear"*

Ask: *What does* **animate** *mean? It means "to make alive." What does* **clarify** *mean? It means "to make clear."*

Model

Use BLM 33, Row 1–2.

Say: *I read the word part* **agit–**. *I can add the suffix* **–ate**. *I can put this all together to create the word* **agitate**. *The word* **agitate** *means "to make nervous." Now, I read the word part* **noti–**. *I can add the suffix* **–fy**. *I can put this all together to create the word* **notify.** *The word* **notify** *means "to make information." You can use the suffix* **–ate** *and suffix* **–fy** *to understand the meaning of a word.*

Lesson Objectives

- Recognize and decode common suffixes.
- Recognize that suffixes placed at the end of a root/base word change the meaning of the word.

Metacognitive Strategy
- Selective Auditory Attention
- Use Deductive Thinking
- Generalize a Rule

Academic Language
- word ending, different meaning, suffix, base word, root word.
- Note: When using Latin-based suffixes, the base word is called a root word.

Additional Materials
- Blackline Master 33

Pre-Assess
Student's ability to recognize the end of a word as a clue to word meaning Student's ability to recognize a base or root word as the part of the word that contains meaning and can stand alone.

Practice

Use BLM 33, Row 3–4.

Say: *Let's read the word* **glory.** *I can change the letter* **y** *to an* **i** *and add the suffix* **–fy.** *I can put this all together to create the word* **glorify.** *The word* **glorify** *means "to make into praise." Now, let's read the word part* **satis–.** *I can add the suffix* **–fy.** *I can put this all together to create the word* **satisfy.** *The word* **satisfy** *means "to make content." You can use the suffix* **–fy** *to understand the meaning of a word.*

Apply
Blend Words
Use BLM 33, Row 5–6.

Say: *You can read the word part* **terri–.** *You can add the suffix* **–fy.** *You can put this all together to create the word* **terrify.** *The word* **terrify** *means "to make frightened." Now, you can read the word part* **beauti–.** *You can add the suffix* **–fy.** *You can put this all together to create the word* **beautify.** *The word* **beautify** *means "to make beautiful." You can use the suffix* **–fy** *to understand the meaning of a word.*

Conclusion

Ask: *What did we learn today? We learned that when we add the suffix* **–ate** *or* **–fy** *to the end of a word, it changes the meaning of the word. The suffix* **–ate** *and* **–fy** *both mean "to make."*

Home Connection
Ask students to practice adding **–ate** and **–fy** to the end of words and to understand the meaning of the new word. Ask students to identify other words that have the suffix **–ate** or **–fy** with a family member.

✔ **Formative Assessment**

If the student completes each task correctly, proceed to the next skill in the sequence. If not, refer to suggested intervention 2.

Did the student…?	Intervention 2
Recognize and identify the end of a word?	• Point directly to the end of the word. Say this is the end of the word____ or the last part of the word____. Point to the beginning and say, this is the beginning or the first part of the word
Understand the meaning of –ate and –fy?	• Create a two-column chart and have students sort –ate and –fy words into the two columns.
Repeat words and phrases when asked?	• Point to the word and have students echo-read, then read it on their own while pointing to the word

Name _____ **Date** _____

1. MODEL

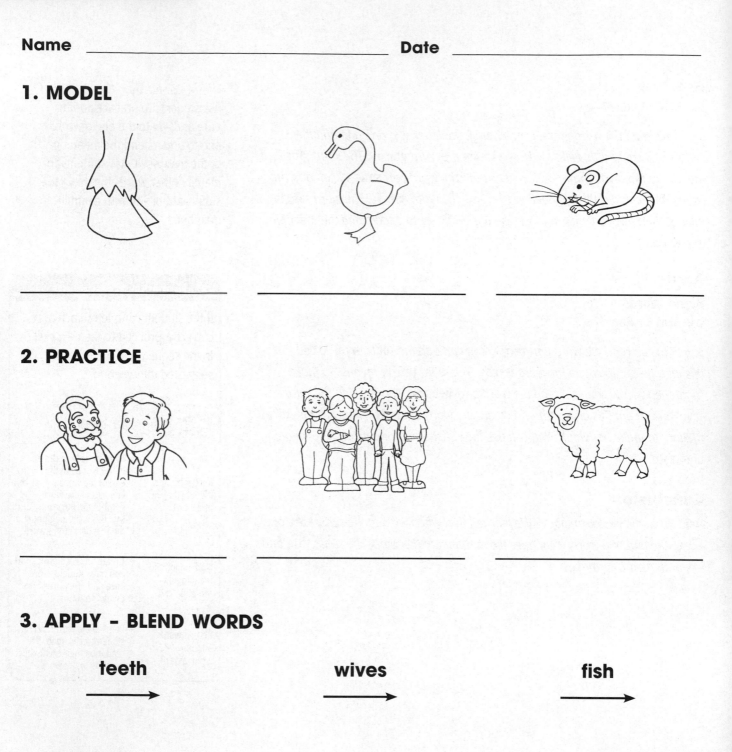

_____   _____   _____

2. PRACTICE

_____   _____   _____

3. APPLY - BLEND WORDS

teeth   **wives**   **fish**

→   →   →

4. SPELLING

_____

_____

_____

Name _____ **Date** _____

1. MODEL

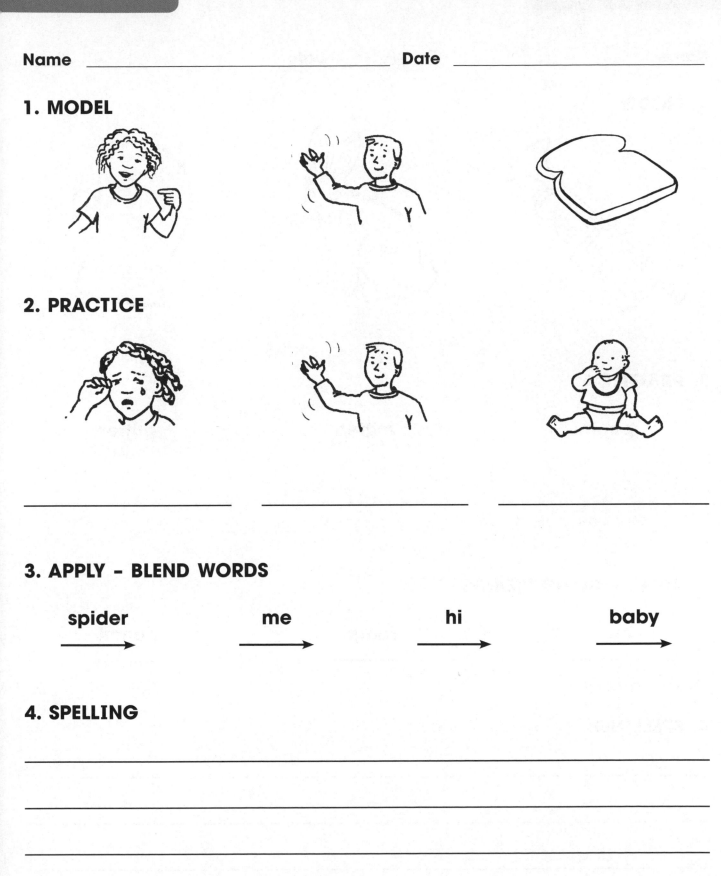

2. PRACTICE

3. APPLY - BLEND WORDS

spider →   me →   hi →   baby →

4. SPELLING

_____

_____

_____

Name _____ **Date** _____

1. MODEL

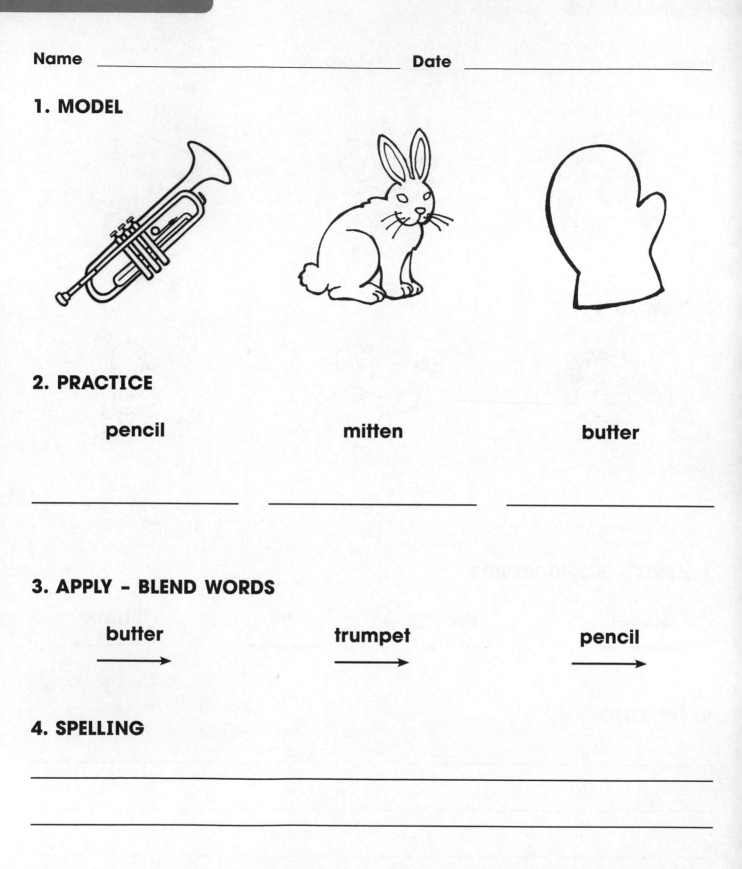

2. PRACTICE

pencil   mitten   butter

_____   _____   _____

3. APPLY - BLEND WORDS

    butter   trumpet   pencil

   →   →   →

4. SPELLING

_____

_____

_____

Name _____ Date _____

1. MODEL

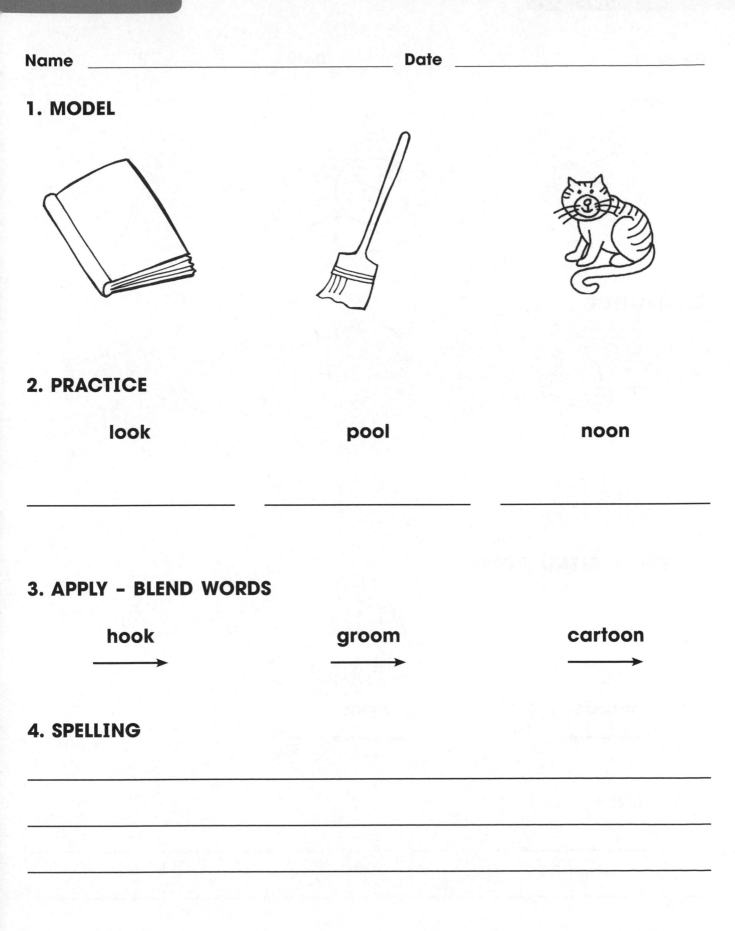

2. PRACTICE

look   pool   noon

_____   _____   _____

3. APPLY - BLEND WORDS

hook   groom   cartoon

———→   ———→   ———→

4. SPELLING

_____

_____

_____

Name _____   **Date** _____

1. MODEL

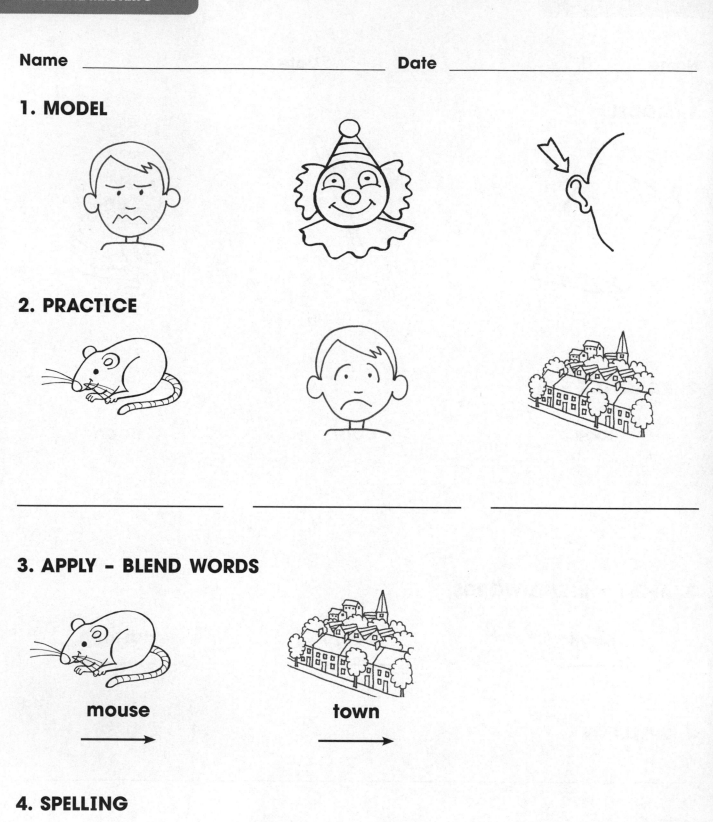

2. PRACTICE

_____   _____   _____

3. APPLY - BLEND WORDS

mouse

→

town

→

4. SPELLING

_____

_____

_____

Name _____ **Date** _____

1. MODEL

2. PRACTICE

_____ _____

3. APPLY - BLEND WORDS

oil →   joy →

4. SPELLING

_____

_____

_____

Name _____ **Date** _____

1. MODEL

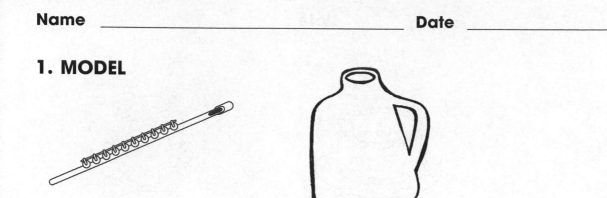

flute   jug

2. PRACTICE

_____   _____

3. APPLY - BLEND WORDS

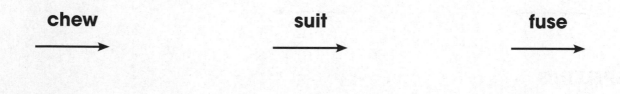

chew   suit   fuse

4. SPELLING

_____

_____

_____

Name _____   **Date** _____

1. MODEL

2. PRACTICE

_____   _____   _____

3. APPLY - BLEND WORDS

here   **cheer**   **fear**   **hear**

→   →   →   →

4. SPELLING

_____

_____

_____

Name _____ **Date** _____

1. MODEL

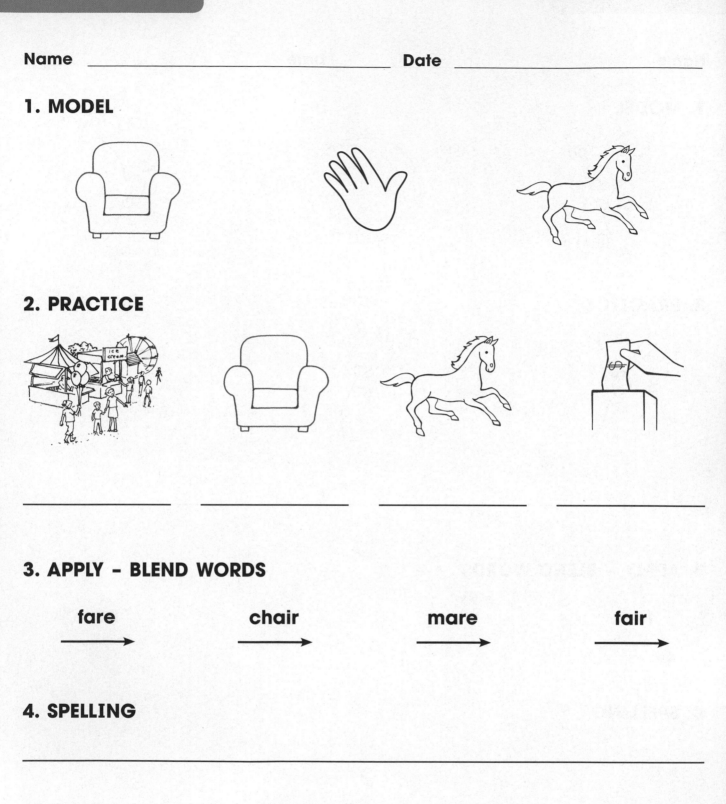

2. PRACTICE

_____   _____   _____   _____

3. APPLY - BLEND WORDS

fare   **chair**   **mare**   **fair**

→   →   →   →

4. SPELLING

_____

_____

_____

Name _____ **Date** _____

1. MODEL

2. PRACTICE

_____   _____   _____

3. APPLY - BLEND WORDS

reptile   invade   landscape
⟶   ⟶   ⟶

4. SPELLING

_____

_____

_____

Name _____ **Date** _____

1. MODEL

2. PRACTICE

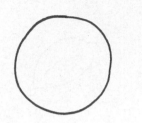

_____ _____

3. APPLY - BLEND WORDS

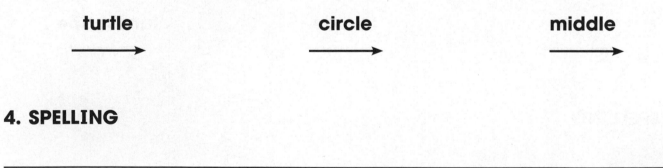

turtle circle middle

4. SPELLING

_____

_____

_____

Name _____ **Date** _____

1. MODEL

sing   sing_____

teach   teach_____

2. PRACTICE

collect   collect_____

paint   paint_____

_____   _____

3. APPLY - BLEND WORDS

act
⟶

actor
⟶

4. SPELLING

_____

_____

_____

Name _____ **Date** _____

1. MODEL

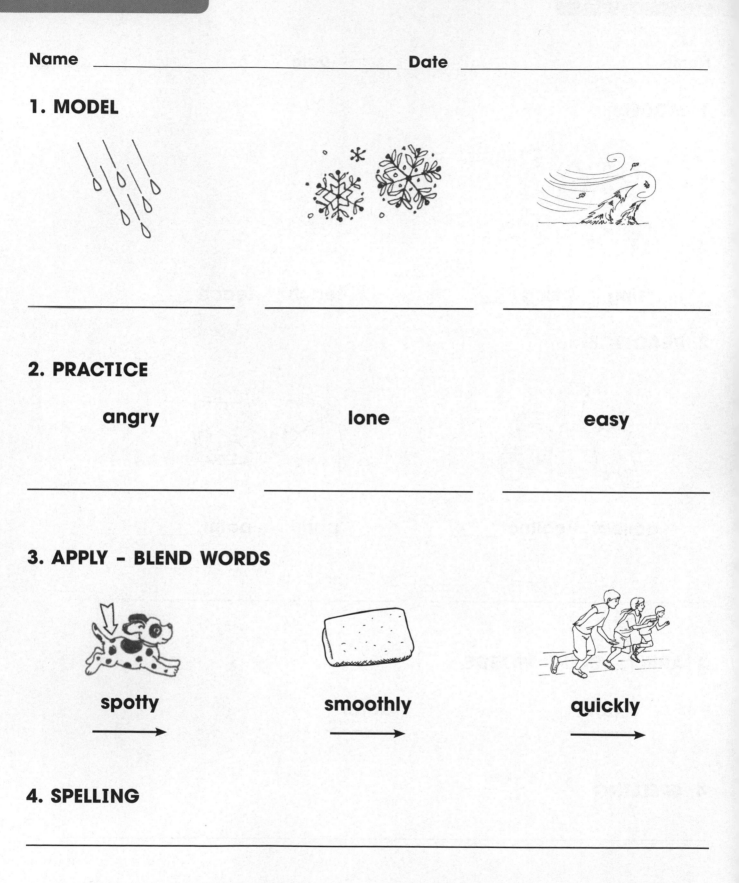

_____   _____   _____

2. PRACTICE

angry   **lone**   **easy**

_____   _____   _____

3. APPLY - BLEND WORDS

spotty   **smoothly**   **quickly**

4. SPELLING

_____

_____

_____

Name _____ Date _____

Directions: Add the prefix *re–*. Then write the new word.

MODEL

1. name _____name _____

PRACTICE

2. write _____write _____

3. fresh _____fresh _____

4. visit _____visit _____

APPLY

5. open _____open _____

6. state _____state _____

7. load _____load _____

Name _____ Date _____

Directions: Add the prefixes *un–* or *non–*.

MODEL

1. lock   _____lock

PRACTICE

2. able   _____able

3. aware   _____aware

4. stop   _____stop

APPLY

5. available   _____available

6. tie   _____tie

7. sense   _____sense

Name _____   Date _____

Directions: Add the suffixes –*ful* or –*less*.

MODEL

1. harm   harmful   harm   harmless

PRACTICE

2. law   law_____   law   law_____

3. care   care_____   care   care_____

4. mercy   merci_____   mercy   merci_____

APPLY

5. sorrow   sorrow_____   defense   defense_____

6. plenty   plenti_____   power   power_____

7. power   power_____   motion   motion_____

Name _____ **Date** _____

Directions: Add the suffixes –*like* or –*ish*.

MODEL

1. home   home_____

PRACTICE

2. life   life_____

3. book   book_____

APPLY

4. tickle   tickl_____

5. child   child_____

Write a word with the suffix –*like*. _____

Name _____ **Date** _____

Directions: Add the suffixes –*ways* or –*ward*.

MODEL

   1. side   side_____

PRACTICE

   2. east   east_____

   3. north   north_____

APPLY

   4. home   home_____

   5. south   south_____

Write a new word that you will make with the suffix –*ward*. _____

Name _____ **Date** _____

Directions: Add prefixes *de–* or *dis–*. Then write the new word.

MODEL

1. belief   _____belief   _____

PRACTICE

2. value   _____value   _____

3. form   _____form   _____

4. code   _____code   _____

APPLY

5. like   _____like   _____

6. honest   _____honest   _____

7. connect   _____connect   _____

Name _____ **Date** _____

Directions: Add the prefix *mis–*. Then write the new word.

MODEL

1. treat   _____treat   _____

PRACTICE

2. dial   _____dial   _____

3. judge   _____judge   _____

4. print   _____print   _____

APPLY

5. lead   _____lead   _____

6. direct   _____direct   _____

7. understand   _____understand   _____

Name _____ **Date** _____

Directions: Add prefixes *trans–* or *inter–*. Then write the new word.

MODEL

1. state   _____state   _____

PRACTICE

2. port   _____port   _____

3. action   _____action   _____

4. form   _____form   _____

APPLY

5. national   _____national   _____

6. office   _____office   _____

7. city   _____city   _____

Name _____ **Date** _____

Directions: Add suffixes *–ment* or *–tion*. Then write the new word.

MODEL

1. adopt   **adopt**_____   _____

PRACTICE

2. develop   **develop**_____   _____

3. except   **except**_____   _____

4. object   **object**_____   _____

APPLY

5. announce   **announce**_____   _____

6. arrange   **arrange**_____   _____

7. move   **move**_____   _____

Name _____ **Date** _____

Directions: Add the prefix *anti–*. Then write the new word.

MODEL

1. anxiety   _____anxiety   _____

PRACTICE

2. freeze   _____freeze   _____

3. body   _____body   _____

APPLY

4. theft   _____theft   _____

5. venom   _____venom   _____

What word could you add the prefix *anti–* to? Write it here.

_____

Name _____ **Date** _____

Directions: Add the prefix *sub-*. Then write the new word.

MODEL

1. merge   _____merge   _____

PRACTICE

2. due   _____due   _____

3. marine   _____marine   _____

APPLY

4. way   _____way   _____

5. topic   _____topic   _____

Name _____ **Date** _____

Directions: Add the prefixes *in–*, *im–* or *ir–*. Then write the new word.

MODEL

1. correct _____correct _____

PRACTICE

2. perfect _____perfect _____

3. active _____active _____

APPLY

4. regular _____regular _____

5. relevant _____relevant _____

Name _____ **Date** _____

MODEL

Directions: Underline the suffix.

1. sensible   **detachable**   **removable**

PRACTICE

Directions: Underline the suffix.

2. respectable   **horrible**   **terrible**

3. visible   **incredible**

APPLY

Directions: Add the suffix.

4. accept_____   **suggest**_____

5. access_____   **renew**_____   **detach**_____

Write your own word with the suffix *–ible* or *–able*. _____

Name _____ Date _____

Directions: Add the suffixes *–ant* or *–ent*. Then write the new word.

MODEL

1. depend   **depend_____**   _____

PRACTICE

2. assist   **assist_____**   _____

3. absorb   **absorb_____**   _____

APPLY

4. contest   **contest_____**   _____

5. differ   **differ_____**   _____

Write your own word adding *–ent* or *–ant* to change the meaning of the word.

_____

Name _____ Date _____

Directions: Add the suffixes *-ous*, *-eous* or *-ious*. Then write the new word.

MODEL

1. joy   joy_____   _____

PRACTICE

2. mystery   myster_____   _____

3. ceremony   ceremon_____   _____

4. glory   glor_____   _____

APPLY

5. advantage   advantag_____   _____

6. gas   gas_____   _____

7. courtesy   courte_____   _____

Name _____ Date _____

Directions: Add the suffixes *-ive*, *-active* or *-itive*. Then write the new word.

MODEL

1. protect   protect_____   _____

PRACTICE

2. add   add_____   _____

3. define   defin_____   _____

4. compete   compet_____   _____

APPLY

5. imagine   imagin_____   _____

6. compare   compar_____   _____

7. cure   cure_____   _____

Name _____ Date _____

Directions: Add the suffixes *–ology*, *–graphic* or *–graphy*. Then write the new word.

MODEL

1. geo   geo_____   _____

PRACTICE

2. bio   bio_____   _____

3. photo   photo_____   _____

4. video   video_____   _____

APPLY

5. zoo   zoo_____   _____

6. ocean   ocean_____   _____

7. criminal   criminal_____   _____

Name _____ **Date** _____

Directions: Add the suffixes –*phobia* or –*scope*. Then write the new word.

MODEL

1. tele   tele_____   _____

PRACTICE

2. aqua   aqua_____   _____

3. claustro   claustro_____   _____

4. arachno   arachno_____   _____

APPLY

5. night   night_____   _____

6. stetho   stetho_____   _____

7. peri   peri_____   _____

Name _____ Date _____

Directions: Add the suffixes *–ory*, or *–ist*. Then write the new word.

MODEL

   1. sense   sens_____   _____

   2. cycle   cycl_____   _____

PRACTICE

   3. supervisory   _____

   4. chemist   _____

APPLY

   5. advise   advis_____   _____

   6. essay   essay_____   _____

Name _____ Date _____

Directions: Add the suffixes –*ate*, or –*fy*. Then write the new word.

MODEL

1. agit_____   _____

2. noti_____   _____

PRACTICE

3. glory_____   _____

4. satis_____   _____

APPLY

5. terri_____   _____

6. beauti_____   _____